Greener Buildings
Environmental impact
of property

Stuart Johnson
with contributions from

Brian Carter
Colin Ferguson
Jagjit Singh
Edward Sutherland
Andrew Wilkes

150th YEAR
MACMILLAN

First published 1993 by
THE MACMILLAN PRESS LTD
Houndmills, Basingstoke, Hampshire RG21 2XS
and London
Companies and representatives
throughout the world

ISBN 0–333–57453–2 (hardcover)
ISBN 0–333–57454–0 (paperback)

A catalogue record for this book is available
from the British Library.

Printed in Hong Kong

Contents

Foreword   ix

1   Introduction
Stuart Johnson   1

      1.1   Aims of the book   1
      1.2   Structure of the book   2
      1.3   Using the book   4
      1.4   Notes on contributors   5

2   Environmental Issues
Stuart Johnson   8

      2.1   Introduction   8
      2.2   Ozone depletion   9
      2.3   Ozone depletion and buildings   10
      2.4   Global warming   12
      2.5   Global warming and buildings   14
      2.6   Acid rain   15
      2.7   Acid rain and buildings   16
      2.8   Neighbourhood and internal environment issues   16
      2.9   Summary   17

3   Site Hazards
Colin Ferguson   20

      3.1   Introduction   20
      3.2   Potentially contaminated land   20
      3.3   Landfill gas   26
      3.4   Indoor radon and lung cancer   30
      3.5   Overhead power lines   37
      3.6   Summary   39

4   Architecture and Landscape
Brian Carter   **45**

    4.1   Introduction   45
    4.2   Site planning   45
    4.3   Orientation   46
    4.4   The characteristics of materials   47
    4.5   The building envelope   49
    4.6   Building systems   53
    4.7   The design of the skin of the building   56
    4.8   Acoustics   59
    4.9   Performance   61
    4.10 Summary   63

5   Energy Efficiency
Stuart Johnson and Andrew Wilkes   **67**

    5.1   Introduction   67
    5.2   Benefits   68
    5.3   Thermal insulation   69
    5.4   Local materials   73
    5.5   'Hidden' energy costs   74
    5.6   Design life of buildings   74
    5.7   Out-of-town schemes   75
    5.8   Energy savings in building systems and services 75
    5.9   Environmental moderating systems   77
    5.10 A holistic approach   79
    5.11 Buildings in equilibrium   81
    5.12 Life cycle costing   82
    5.13 Summary   85

6   Building Materials
Stuart Johnson   **89**

    6.1   Introduction   89
    6.2   Tropical hardwoods   90
    6.3   Chlorofluorocarbons   92
    6.4   Asbestos   93
    6.5   Paints   94
    6.6   Timber treatments   97
    6.7   Formaldehyde   98
    6.8   Recycled materials   99
    6.9   Summary   100

7 **Engineering Services**
Andrew Wilkes   104

      7.1   Introduction   104
      7.2   Environmental aspects of the building   105
      7.3   Environmental performance   106
      7.4   Control of personal environments   109
      7.5   Thermal comfort criteria   110
      7.6   Ventilation and indoor air quality   111
      7.7   Heating/ventilating/air-conditioning (HVAC)
             systems   114
      7.8   Summary   120

8 **Building Biology and Health**
Jagjit Singh   122

      8.1   Introduction   122
      8.2   Building environments   123
      8.3   Biological decay   125
      8.4   Biological health hazards   136
      8.5   Environmental assessment   138
      8.6   Environmental control   139
      8.7   Summary   140

9 **Environmental Law**
T Edward Sutherland   144

      9.1   Introduction   144
      9.2   The planning stage   145
      9.3   Contaminated land   148
      9.4   Construction   150
      9.5   Occupied buildings   156
      9.6   Demolition   157
      9.7   Future developments   157
      9.8   Summary   158

10 **Environmental Assessment**
Stuart Johnson   160

      10.1   Introduction   160
      10.2   BREEAM systems   161
      10.3   Environmental surveys   165
      10.4   Environmental impact assessments   167
      10.5   Energy labelling   167
      10.6   Product labelling   169
      10.7   Summary   169

11   Conclusions
     Stuart Johnson   **172**

     11.1   Introduction   172
     11.2   Environmental issues   173
     11.3   Site hazards   174
     11.4   Architecture and landscape   175
     11.5   Energy efficiency   175
     11.6   Building materials   177
     11.7   Engineering services   178
     11.8   Building biology and health   179
     11.9   Environmental law   180
     11.10 Environmental assessment   180
     11.11 Overall conclusions   181

Index   183

Foreword

Heightened concern about the threat of environmental catastrophe has coincided with a downturn in the fortunes of those involved in the property market and the construction industry. There is no doubt that the present over-supply in the market is enabling occupiers to exercise their preferences by choosing the buildings that are both environmentally friendly and cheaper to run. Stuart Johnson's book is therefore not only valuable, pulling together the many environmental threads that relate to property and construction, but timely.

The agents of change are often described as the carrot and the stick but, in its ability to change course, the construction industry is more like a super-tanker than a donkey; its enormous size will make it slow to change direction even when the helm is hard over. Many believe that we will not see environmental concerns leading to action unless a legislative stick is applied to the construction industry. Statutory regulation is important but at the moment it tends to apply only to new buildings. On the other hand, information and a will to take action can affect choices in respect of both new and existing buildings. I hope that this book will provide those who feel like nibbling at the carrot of a better environment with the information they need.

It is a similar wish that has motivated The Royal Institution of Chartered Surveyors to take a keen interest in the subject of the environment by exposing members to issues of current concern and by talking to government on environmental issues affecting property and construction. The aim is to raise interest in the subject and point the direction in which the property profession can meet existing and expected demand for practical and unbiased advice.

There has been much research into the way in which buildings affect our environment. This book lists many of the current references. In bringing together contributions from a wide variety of experts it is my hope that it will enable enlightened self-interest to grow among property professionals.

This book will help those who wish to respond to market require-ments, develop their understanding of environmental issues and adapt their services to provide us with, and help us occupy, greener buildings.

Ted Watts
President, The Royal Institution
of Chartered Surveyors, 1991–2
and Chairman, Watts & Partners

1 Introduction
Stuart Johnson

1.1 Aims of the book

Even as recently as the late 1980s, green issues were almost exclusively the province of pressure groups and few organisations in the public or private sectors of the economy had given thought to the environmental impact of their operations. This is no longer the case. Environmental issues are a mainstream concern which has been the subject of a great deal of debate; consideration is even being given to changing the methods by which we measure the economic growth of both nations and companies, because unless protection of the rain forests, purity of water and air and so on are given a value it is unlikely that growth will be sustainable. Increased concern about the quality of our environment has influenced property and construction too, but there is little guidance on how to translate this concern into action. This book aims to meet that need. The contributors' objectives are simple: to produce a guide to the environmental impact of buildings which can be applied to specific properties at any stage in their life by anyone with an interest in them.

It is important to appreciate that the contributors have not tried to push forward the boundaries of scientific knowledge, but instead have aimed to present existing research in a manner which can be used easily. Each chapter includes a further reading list. The main reason for this is that product development, regulations and research are changing rapidly in this field, so it is not desirable to rely exclusively on this book.

A building's environmental impact extends from global factors such as ozone depletion to the quality of the environment inside the property. These impacts arise from decisions made at all stages of a building's life, including materials manufacture, site selection, design, construction, occupation and ultimately demolition. There are, of course, other environmental impacts that are not directly related to our use of buildings but which arise from organisations' other activi-

1

ties, such as the creation and disposal of waste from manufacturing processes in various forms. These lie outside the scope of this book.

Returning to our use of buildings, the recurring theme is our use of various resources in a way which does not prejudice the health of people, plants, animals and the environment unduly. It is acknowledged that our construction and occupation of buildings will continue, and with it our use of resources, but that the amount and method of consumption will have to change. Our future is likely to be characterised by a more cautious approach to resource use and greater attention to all facets of our environment. Each of us is likely to be driven towards this for different reasons. Some will see greater concern for the environment as a way of reducing costs and the most obvious vehicle for this is energy saving. Others will perceive that buildings with better than average environmental performance will be more desirable and therefore more valuable and perhaps easier to let or sell. Lastly, regulations and legislation will make environmental concern less and less discretionary. Law is likely to be affected by changes in British legislation, and implementation of European Commission directives and international agreements, such as the one proposed on the use of fossil fuels.

As mentioned earlier, environmental impact arises from all stages of a building's life and for this reason a contribution is made by all parties involved in property. In its simplest form, the only party with an interest in a building will be an owner occupier, but in practice the situation is often more complex. Materials manufacturers, contractors, architects, surveyors and other professionals, financiers, funding institutions, developers, occupiers and students all play a part, as do bodies representing professional and other groups, research centres and government. This book was written to help these people to mitigate the environmental impact of their buildings, particularly for small and medium-sized commercial buildings, but almost all of the principles apply equally well to other building sizes, uses and types.

Whilst this book aims to introduce the main environmental issues, care must be taken when applying the advice in specific cases. Environmental issues are complicated and interrelated and, where there is any doubt, specialist advice must be sought.

1.2 Structure of the book

This section explains the structure of the book, which comprises chapters on specific environmental issues written by specialists within those fields. In broad terms, the chapters can be divided into three. The early chapters deal with strategic issues like site selection and the position and configuration of the building. Later chapters deal with the more detailed decisions which are necessary for the refinement of a proposal from conceptual to detailed design. The concluding chapters give an overview of the environment from different perspectives, such as environmental law.

Chapter 2, on environmental issues, sets the book in context by introducing the main issues of global concern, ozone depletion, global warming and acid rain. Their relevance to buildings is explored with particular reference to our use of the man-made chemicals, chlorofluorocarbons, and the burning of fossil fuels to create energy. Quality of the local and the internal environments is also dealt with. The book then goes on to review the environmental impacts of sites, especially redevelopment sites that in the past may have been put to contaminative use. Chapter 3 looks not only at contaminated land but also at the special problems posed by landfill gases and radon gas. Lastly, the possible implications of close proximity to high-voltage, overhead power lines is reviewed. Chapter 4 sets out the strategic decisions regarding the design of buildings and their relationship with and impact on the environment. Many significant environmental aspects are determined at this stage, including the building orientation, the impact on micro-climate, fundamental decisions arising from the choice of materials and building systems, and so on.

Having built up an awareness of the principal environmental issues and dealt with the strategic issues arising from the site and conceptual design, detailed attention needs to be given to the building fabric and its services installation. Chapter 5 considers energy efficiency of both the building fabric and services and looks at ways of improving efficiency at the design stage and during the life of a building. Particular emphasis is placed upon the need to examine total energy consumption over a building's life, perhaps using life cycle cost techniques, rather than studying each aspect in isolation.

The selection of building materials affects the environment, both externally and within buildings. Chapter 6 introduces the concepts which should govern the specification of materials and gives specific guidance on a number of products. In particular, advice is given on the use of timber, chlorofluorocarbons, asbestos, solvent and lead-based paints, timber treatments, formaldehyde and the use of recycled materials. The significance of building materials' impact should not be underestimated in creating a healthy environment. Chapter 7 expounds upon individual engineering services and explains the differing types of systems that are currently available and the impact of each upon the building's form and shape. The last issue dealt with under the heading of detailed building design is building biology and health, in Chapter 8. There are many biological aspects of the internal environment which can affect health and examples are insects, pests and micro-organisms.

The concluding chapters are relevant to both strategic and the more detailed property decisions. Chapter 9 covers environmental law from a British perspective, although the European Community legal framework is also dealt with. Regulations and legislation relating to all phases of a building's life are covered, from acquisition to demolition. Chapter 10 sets out the ways in which a building may be environmentally assessed. It sets the parameters for the creation of a bespoke assessment and introduces the proprietary methods such as BREEAM and the energy labelling systems. The final chapter offers conclusions for the subject matter included in each of the preceding chapters, as well as overall conclusions.

1.3 Using the book

The book has been structured to allow information to be used in a number of different ways. In general terms, the order of the chapters follows the decision-making process required for a development scheme. The previous section of this chapter explores the book's structure in more detail. Thus, the most obvious application of the book is to enable consideration of the environmental performance of proposed buildings. The introduction to Chapter 10 offers one way of formulating an environmental strategy by producing the policy based on the information given in this guide and other references. Ideally, this would need to be applied to all phases of the project, from feasibility study to completion.

Whilst there is arguably less scope for modifying the environmental impact of an existing property than a proposed building, there are still many things that can be done. Some of the environmental assessment methods described in Chapter 10 apply to our existing stock, as do comments in that chapter about bespoke assessments. Existing buildings constrain the ways in which environmental impact can be minimised; for example, there is much more scope to obtain maximum benefit from solar gains and associated natural heating when deciding on the orientation of a new building than in modifying an existing one. The need to identify practical solutions which are tailored to specific buildings and the needs of those that have an interest in them is especially relevant in this case.

Another way in which this book can be used is to establish an environmental policy to govern the acquisition and management of an organisation's entire property portfolio. Many organisations, including retailers and institutional investors, have a desire to minimise the environmental impact of the buildings which they occupy or own. An environmental policy covering such things as the use of chlorofluoro-carbons and the measures to be taken to ensure a healthy internal environment are a means of doing this. The last use envisaged for this book is to act as a source of information on specific issues, for example the environmental performance of paints or the issues to be addressed when thermal insulation materials are chosen.

1.4 Notes on contributors

Brian Carter Dip Arch M Arch RIBA

Brian Carter is an architect working at Arup Associates in London who has been involved in the design of a number of award-winning build-ings. He has also contributed to several books as well as professional journals including the *Architectural Review, World Architecture* and the journals of the RIBA and AIA.

   As a full-time tutor, RIBA external examiner and visiting critic, he has participated in educational programmes at universities in Europe and at the University of California, Berkeley and Rhode Island School of Design in the United States. In 1987 he was the Chettle Visiting Fellow in Architecture at the University of Sydney. Brian Carter is a fellow of the Royal Society of Arts.

Colin Ferguson BSc PhD FGS FIMM MIWEM M Inst WM

Professor Colin Ferguson holds a BSc (first class honours) and PhD in Geology from Nottingham University where he subsequently taught for ten years before moving to the University of Kansas as Associate Professor. He returned to the UK as Professor of Geology in London University and Head of Department at Birkbeck College. He later became a founder director of Chemex International plc, and an en-vironmental consultant. He is now head of the Centre for Research into the Built Environment at the Nottingham Trent University. A fellow of the Institution of Mining and Metallurgy, and member of both the Institution of Water and Environmental Management and the Institute of Wastes Management, his major interests are in contaminated land, waste management, and environmental risk and impact assessment. Currently he serves on the Department of the Environment Study Group on contaminated land risk assessment, and the expert panel for the Institute of Environmental Assessment. He has published about 80 papers and abstracts in the scientific literature, and has presented his work at numerous international conferences.

Stuart Johnson BSc ARICS Dip Proj Man

Stuart Johnson is a chartered building surveyor and project manager. He is an associate at the consultants, Watts & Partners, and is the firm's spokesman on the environment. Stuart developed and launched the practice's range of environmental services which are based upon an especially designed computer database. He regularly undertakes environmental surveys of existing buildings and acts as an environmental consultant for new construction. In addition, he has helped clients to develop environmental policies for their property portfolios and has been commissioned to carry out work for research bodies. Stuart regularly presents papers on environmental issues at seminars and conferences including the RICS Building Surveyors' National Briefing, April 1992. He writes widely on environmental topics.

Jagjit Singh BSc MSc PhD AIWSc

Jagjit Singh was awarded first class degrees from Kurukshetra University specialising in mycology and plant pathology, and his doctorate by the University of London in 1986 for work on the biological control of fungi. He is an associate member of the Institute of Wood Science. His post-doctoral fellowship continued his research into competitive colonisation of crops by fungi which he followed as a research officer funded by MAFF studying mycotoxigenic fungi and their relations with other saprophytic micro-organisms. He joined Hutton + Rostron in 1987 as Principal Scientist responsible for environmental investigations and worked for clients in the control of timber decay, biological hazards in buildings, and consultancy in biodeterioration generally. He is a member of the Society of British Plant Pathology, the British Mycological Society and the British Ecological Society. He is the editor of a book called *Building Mycology* to be published by E & F N Spon, an imprint of Chapman & Hall.

He is a director of Hutton + Rostron Environmental Investigations Limited and of Fungal Control Systems Limited.

Edward Sutherland

Edward Sutherland is a partner in London solicitors Boodle Hatfield and is a member of the United Kingdom Environmental Law Association. Admitted as a solicitor in 1972, he has worked both in industry and private practice, including ten years with Mobil Oil Company Limited as a senior solicitor in their in-house legal department. Since joining Boodle Hatfield in 1987, he has played an important role in developing the firm's Environmental Law Group. His published works include an article in the *Solicitors' Journal* on the Environmental Protection Act 1990, and a series of articles for that journal on air and noise pollution. He is the co-author with a colleague at Boodle Hatfield of a paper in the journal, *Practical Law for Companies*, on waste disposal on land. He has conducted seminars on the Environmental Protection Act 1990. In 1991, he addressed a session of the Institution of Mechanical Engineers' Conference, Eurotech 91, on the use of 'best available technology' as a means of controlling pollution. Other issues with which he is currently involved include waste disposal on land and the new waste management regime established under the Environmental Protection Act.

Eur Ing Andrew Wilkes BSc CEng MIEE MInstE MCIBSE MIEEE ACIArb FIHospE FInstD FFB

Andrew Wilkes has long practised the provision of healthy, responsible buildings. His belief in aesthetic proportion enhances architectural judgement whilst his holistic approach addresses the fundamental issues of concern in today's buildings. He is a partner of Andrew Wilkes Management, a firm created to specialise in the efficient design, management and cost control of mechanical and electrical environmental engineering systems; he is also a founding partner of Facilities Diagnostics – an environmental psychology consultancy with offices in the US and Europe.

Andrew Wilkes is an occasional lecturer at the European Centre for Management in Brussels; a past visiting lecturer at the University of Bath, School of Architecture; and a past lecturer in the electrical aspects of building engineering services at the Polytechnic of the South Bank. He has also presented papers at conferences, seminars and professional institution meetings together with articles in journals and other printed documents. His knowledge and understanding of regulations and standards enables expert witness and arbitration representation to be carried out and he sits on many national committees determining the future direction of the profession and industry.

2 Environmental Issues
Stuart Johnson

2.1 Introduction

There is a story of an advertising campaign heralding the launch of a new model by one of the leading motor manufacturers which announced proudly that the car's engine would not harm the ozone layer; this is a truism – to know why is to have an appreciation of the main environmental issues and reference to this chapter is probably not necessary, but if not then read on.

Whilst this story is not necessarily true, it does illustrate the widespread misunderstanding about the environment. Any attempts to improve the environmental performance of our buildings requires a clear understanding of the principal issues. Ozone depletion, global warming, tropical hardwoods, acid rain, chlorofluorocarbons, the list seems interminable but these phenomena, and the way in which they relate to each other, are straightforward.

This chapter aims to give a concise description of ozone depletion, global warming and acid rain as well as introducing the neighbourhood issues and factors which determine the quality of the internal environment. Having an appreciation of these fundamental environmental topics is a prerequisite for effective decision making to enhance the environmental performance of our buildings; there is no simple checklist of standard solutions which are universally applicable. To be practical and viable all decisions should take into account a number of factors, including the aims of occupiers and owners, whether it is an existing building or a proposed scheme, and also the type of building. As an example, in general terms energy efficiency should be enhanced, but this is not always the case. Some large, modern warehouses contain computer-controlled storage systems with few people using the building on a regular basis. Therefore, it is conceivable that more energy will be consumed in producing, transporting and installing thermal insulation to the external envelope of an unheated building than will ever be wasted through heat loss.

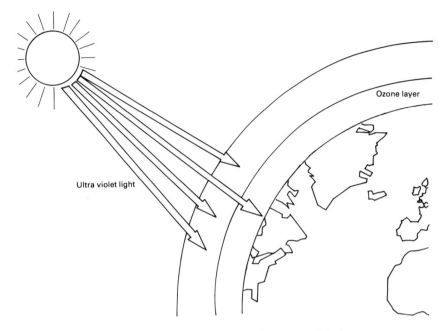

Figure 2.1   The ozone layer – the natural balance.

2.2 Ozone depletion

Readers of the introduction will find the reasons for the advertiser's discomfort in this section.

The earth is protected by a layer of ozone gas at high level in the atmosphere, or stratosphere, which filters almost all of the harmful ultraviolet light from the sun and stops it reaching the earth's surface. This process is shown in Figure 2.1.

Use of the man-made compound chlorofluorocarbon (CFC) is the principal chemical leading to depletion of the ozone layer. When CFCs are discharged to the atmosphere, perhaps as a result of careless maintenance or leakage from equipment, they react with sunlight to produce chlorine. Chlorine destroys ozone by means of a chemical reaction which turns it into oxygen. CFCs are stable compounds and therefore, once released from the atmosphere, they will last for a long time. By this process, the ozone layer is becoming less efficient at screening ultraviolet light, as illustrated by Figure 2.2.

The effect of increased levels of ultraviolet light at the earth's surface could include a higher incidence of skin cancers, cataracts and possibly an adverse effect on human immunity. Furthermore, ozone depletion may reduce crop yields. Uncertainty over the precise nature of the

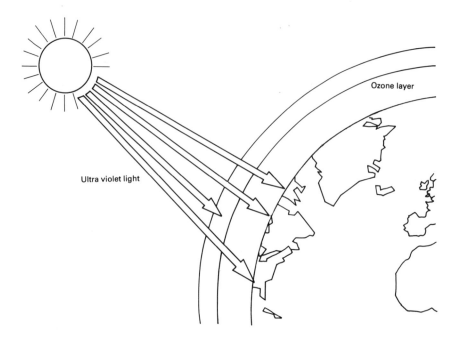

Figure 2.2   The ozone layer – the influence of man.

effects is no justification for failure to address ozone depletion immediately.

The reader will by now appreciate that ozone depletion is triggered by the release of CFCs into the atmosphere and has nothing whatsoever to do with the efficiency of car engines. There are, of course, significant environmental dimensions to our use of petrol and other fossil fuels, particularly global warming and acid rain, and these are explored later in this chapter.

2.3 Ozone depletion and buildings

CFCs are used in a number of building components including some forms of insulation, air conditioning, refrigeration plant and fire-fighting systems as well as some packaging foams, aerosol sprays and soft furnishings.

As CFCs result in depletion of the ozone layer the solution that initially presents itself is to avoid using them. Unfortunately, substitute chemicals have not been developed in all cases. As discussed later in this section, consideration should be given to meeting requirements for insulation, air conditioning and so on by other means, but this is not to say that substitute chemicals are not (or will not become) available. The substitutes will be hydrochlorofluorocarbons (HCFCs) and ultimately hydrofluorocarbons (HFCs). HCFCs are significantly less damaging to the ozone layer than CFCs and are likely to become available in the near future; R22, a HCFC compound, is already available for use in air conditioning plant. HFCs are not harmful to the ozone layer and compounds suitable for widespread substitution are expected to be available by the mid-1990s; R152a is a HFC which is available now and can be used in some refrigeration equipment.

In general terms, CFCs are gradually giving way to HCFCs which are viewed as a stop-gap measure pending the development and launch of HFCs. There are two points worth noting about these alternative chemicals. First, both HCFCs and HFCs are greenhouse gases, albeit to a lesser extent than CFCs. The second point is that some of these new compounds may be less efficient and more toxic than the CFCs which they replace and it is important to appraise their performance before selecting them. The availability of alternatives to CFCs is rapidly changing, so it is important to obtain a clear idea of the current status before making a choice.

International agreements, such as the 1987 Montreal Protocol and its later revisions, aim to reduce emissions of CFCs to the atmosphere by controlling both production and consumption of many CFC compounds. Although there are currently no laws or regulations in Britain controlling the consumption of CFCs, it is reasonable to expect that there will be at some time in the future; already there is a European Commission regulation banning almost all production of CFCs by 1997, and in early 1992 the EC Environment Commissioner proposed that elimination of all ozone-depleting compounds be brought forward to 31 December 1995. Therefore, we must all strive to avoid the use of CFCs, wherever possible, not only to satisfy our concern for the environment but also to reduce the risk of installing equipment which may become obsolete when replacement CFCs are no longer readily available.

There are a number of ways in which the use of CFCs in buildings can be minimised, from substitution of CFCs with another material to adopting a different design solution. An example of the use of another material is by choosing, say, mineral fibre thermal insulation rather than one of the CFC-blown insulants such as extruded polystyrene. The issues involved here are considered more fully in Chapter 6, which discusses building materials. Sometimes simple substitution is not possible, but a different design solution may overcome the need for CFCs. Halon (halogenated hydrocarbon) which is chemically related to CFCs is frequently used as a fire-extinguishing system within computer rooms, as discharge of the gas will not damage computers. Rather than

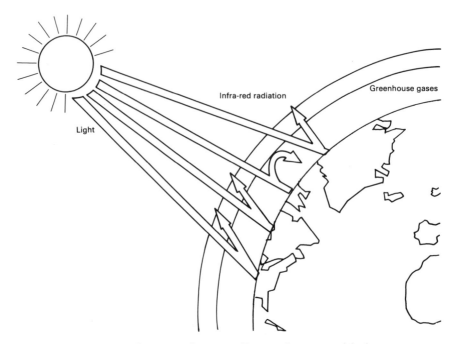

Figure 2.3   The greenhouse effect – the natural balance.

assuming that a halon gas fire-extinguishing system is required, the water resistance of the computer equipment should be checked, as hardware is becoming increasingly resistant and a water sprinkler system may be appropriate.

In certain situations, even bearing in mind the restricted future supply of the compounds, it is considered necessary to specify CFCs. Even where this is the case there is scope for using them more carefully than has been customary. Careful commissioning and maintenance procedures should be adopted, in conjunction with leak detectors, to minimise the risk of discharge of CFCs into the atmosphere.

2.4 Global warming

The earth is covered with a protective blanket of greenhouse gases in the lower atmosphere, or troposphere. These greenhouse gases include carbon dioxide, methane, nitrous oxide and CFCs. As illustrated by Figure 2.3, the gases allow light to reach the earth's surface, but absorb some infra-red radiation. This phenomenon is known as the greenhouse effect because, like a glasshouse, sunlight passes through and it becomes warmer inside than out. Similarly, the blanket of

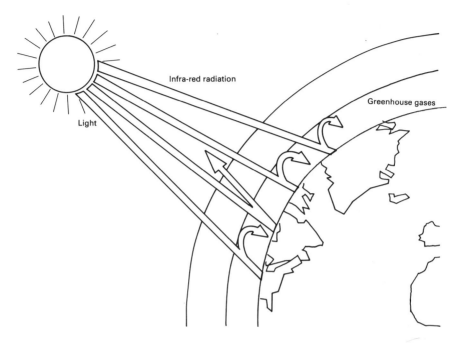

Figure 2.4   The greenhouse effect – the influence of man.

greenhouse gases produces a higher temperature at the earth's surface which is essential to support animal and plant life; without greenhouse gases the earth would be so cold that the oceans would freeze [1].

It is now accepted that because of man's activity, the blanket of greenhouse gases is becoming thicker. This is due to a number of factors including the emission of carbon dioxide when fossil fuels are burnt, the release of CFCs into the atmosphere and methane produced by, amongst other things, intensive agriculture. A thicker layer of greenhouse gases is more efficient at absorbing infra-red radiation, thus increasing temperatures at the earth's surface; this is known as global warming and is illustrated in Figure 2.4.

Whilst it is now commonly accepted that global warming is occurring, there is no consensus on the amount of global warming likely to take place or its time-scale. For these reasons, the effect of a sustained increase in the earth's temperature is a matter for speculation but could include partial melting of the polar ice caps and thermal expansion of the oceans with the loss of low-lying land to the associated flooding. Also, a change in climate would lead to a shift in deserts and fertile areas. It is anticipated that changes in climate will not be restricted to an increase in average temperatures, but will be characterised by more unsettled weather with a greater range of temperatures and rainfall rates. More extreme weather conditions will have a greater effect because, as an example, a surge in sea level as a result of a storm will make flooding much more likely than a simple increase in sea level overall.

2.5 Global warming and buildings

Of the main greenhouse gases currently being emitted, carbon dioxide and CFCs are most directly related to our use of buildings.

So far as carbon dioxide is concerned, this accounts for about one-half of all greenhouse gases being produced and in the UK about 50 per cent of all carbon dioxide emitted is directly related to our use of buildings [2]. In particular, most electricity generation relies upon the burning of fossil fuels. So, whilst in the long term the government may invest in alternative energy sources, those of us with an interest in buildings can help to mitigate global warming now by using energy more efficiently. Many factors influence energy conservation from the degree of thermal insulation to the efficiency of services plant and even the aspect and configuration of the building. Energy is used for heating of space and water, cooling of space, ventilation, lighting, passenger lifts and so on. Obviously, the measures taken to enhance energy efficiency will depend upon the type of building, how it is occupied and whether it is existing or on the drawing board. Chapter 5, on energy efficiency, explores these issues.

Building regulations go some way in controlling the energy efficiency of buildings by setting out the thermal performance to be achieved for various elements of new structures. Inevitably, these controls will become more stringent over time and further legislation is likely. The European Commission is currently considering whether to produce a directive requiring energy certification and it will be interesting to see what becomes of this and other proposed legislation. Controls on the production and consumption of CFCs are also applicable here because the compounds are greenhouse gases as well as having ozone-depleting potential.

The process by which CFCs harm the ozone layer has already been dealt with, but these compounds are also greenhouse gases. Estimates vary, but it is likely that CFCs cause 25 per cent of global warming and, although the actual amounts released are quite small when compared to carbon dioxide, their effect is significant because they are many times more potent in adding to the greenhouse effect – up to 7500 times per unit mass [3]. Therefore, the use of CFCs should be avoided wherever possible, and when their use is essential, care must be taken to specify compounds with a low ozone-depleting factor in conjunc-

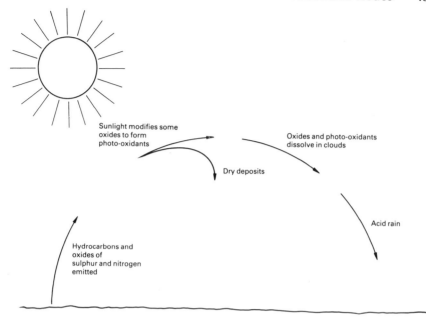

Figure 2.5   Rain – the process of acidification.

tion with operating and maintenance procedures which minimise leakage.

Methane is another greenhouse gas and as it is one of the main constituents of natural gas, there is a need to avoid leaks; a desire to avoid explosion is perhaps a more pressing reason for avoiding a leaking gas supply!

The greenhouse gas nitrous oxide is formed when fossil fuels are burnt. At present, there is little information about its contribution towards global warming, but it is not thought to be a major source.

2.6 Acid rain

The acidity of rainfall is a result of a number of natural occurrences, such as the growth of plants and animals, and man-made sources, such as the burning of fossil fuels. The gases responsible for acidification include sulphur dioxide, nitrogen oxides and hydrocarbons, and in the northern hemisphere, sulphur dioxide is the most significant contributor to acid rain.

The process by which rain becomes more acidic is shown in Figure 2.5. Hydrocarbons and oxides of sulphur and nitrogen are emitted from both natural and man-made sources. Some of these emissions fall near their source as dry deposits and these harm building materials, including stone and metal, trees and crops as well as human health. High concentrations of air-borne sulphur dioxide are detrimental to human health. Sunlight modifies some of the remaining oxides in the air to form photo-oxidants which produce sulphuric and nitric acids. The sulphur and nitrogen oxides, photo-oxidants and so on dissolve in clouds to form acids which fall as acid rain often many thousands of kilometres from the source. These wet deposits increase the acidity of soil and water courses, thus releasing toxic metals from their compounds to poison plants and animals.

2.7 Acid rain and buildings

In the northern hemisphere, sulphur dioxide is the significant contributor to acid rain. In the UK, most sulphur dioxide emissions arise from burning of fossil fuels in power stations. Therefore, maximising energy efficiency of individual buildings will help to reduce acid rain by reducing demand for power. Ways of maximising energy efficiency are given in Chapter 5.

Building materials, especially stone and certain metals, are adversely affected by acid deposition particularly in urban and coastal areas. Current research indicates that oxides of nitrogen and sulphur are responsible for the deterioration of stones and metals, carbon dioxide results in problems with concrete, and ozone and photo-oxidants adversely affect plastics and paints. Car exhausts are thought to be the major contributor to this deterioration in urban areas. Unfortunately, there is no conclusive evidence to prove a link between emissions and deterioration but research is currently underway.

Periodic cleaning to remove the pollutants from facades followed by repointing and other making good of stonework will reduce the risk of future damage. For historic buildings, where considerable expenditure is justified, further protection is available from micro-porous solutions which stabilise the surface of the stone.

2.8 Neighbourhood and internal environment issues

Earlier sections of this chapter have dealt with the issues which affect the global environment but there are other environmental considerations which affect neighbourhoods and the interior of buildings. These are introduced here.

Legionella

There are many strains of the bacteria which cause legionnaires' disease and they are mainly characterised by pneumonia. Whilst the disease is uncommon it can be fatal. Legionella is widespread in natural fresh water and it is, therefore, likely that low concentrations of the bacteria exist in all open water systems including building services. Multiplication of the bacteria will take place in warm water, particularly around 37°C, and where water is stagnant the concentrations of bacteria can reach dangerous levels. Water contaminated in this way is only a risk when dispersed into the atmosphere in small droplets which can be inhaled and cause illness. Depending upon the source, infection can arise within buildings or outside them. Thus, infection by *Legionella pneumophila* is effectively avoided by careful design and regular maintenance of building services. Information on reducing the risk of an outbreak of the disease can be found in Chartered Institution of Building Services Engineers' Guidelines TM13 and the Health and Safety Executive publication HS(G)70 and the accompanying Approved Code of Practice. Further mention of this subject can be found in Chapter 7, on engineering services.

Internal environment

Many factors influence the environment within buildings including the choice of building materials, infestation by insects and other pests, and the efficiency of services equipment.

Solvent-based paints, asbestos and timber treatments are among the building materials which can affect the health of occupants. Chapter 6 explores these issues and identifies the need for a cautious approach to specification. Insects, pests and micro-organisms have health effects, including bronchitis, asthma, allergic alveolitis, endotoxin fever and infection. Chapter 8, on building biology and health, tackles these issues. Lastly, the need to maintain temperature and humidity within normally desirable limits is explored in Chapter 7, on engineering services.

2.9 Summary

- Our use of chlorofluorocarbons (CFCs) is depleting the ozone layer and thus reducing its efficiency at screening the earth from harmful ultraviolet light.
- CFCs should not be used, but where this is not possible or

appropriate, compounds which result in the least harm to the ozone layer should be preferred and measures taken to avoid release to the atmosphere.

- Increased emissions of carbon dioxide, CFCs, methane and other greenhouse gases are resulting in global warming.
- A significant proportion of greenhouse gases arise from electricity generation and we should strive to improve the energy efficiency of our buildings to mitigate global warming.
- Sulphur dioxide is the main cause of acid rain and in the UK over 70 per cent of sulphur dioxide is attributable to power stations. This is another reason for increasing energy efficiency of buildings on environmental grounds.
- The bacteria legionella has an adverse affect on the neighbourhood environment and care must be taken not to create conditions for its release into the atmosphere.
- Building services directly influence the quality of the internal environment. Care must be taken with the original installation and subsequent maintenance that the conditions created fall within normally accepted temperature and humidity limits. Failure to do so can result in a case of sick building syndrome.
- Our choice of building materials affects the internal environment. We should be aware of the health implications of the products which we specify both to the applicators and building users.
- Insects, pests and micro-organisms can affect the health of building occupants. Construction and maintenance should strive to reduce their effect to a minimum.

References

1. R. Baldwin *et al.*, *BREEAM 1/90 – An Environmental Assessment for New Office Designs* (Watford: BRE, 1990).
2. G. Henderson and L. D. Shorrock, *BRE Information Paper 2/90 Greenhouse-gas Emissions and Buildings in the United Kingdom* (Watford: BRE, 1990).
3. Building Research Establishment, *BRE Digest 358 CFCs and Buildings* (Watford: BRE, 1991).

Further Reading

Building Effects Review Group Report, *The Effects of Acid Deposition on Buildings and Building Materials in the United Kingdom* (London: HMSO, 1989).

Building Research Establishment, *BRE Digest 358 CFCs and Buildings* (Watford: BRE, 1991).

B. Evans, 'Trouble in the air – ozone/greenhouse effects', *Architect's Journal* (April 1989), pp. 75–80.

Central Electricity Generating Board, *Acid Rain* (London: CEGB, 1984).

Department of the Environment, *The Effects of Acid Deposition on the Terrestrial Environment in the United Kingdom* (London: HMSO, 1988).

G. Henderson and L. D. Shorrock, *BRE Information Paper 2/90 Greenhouse-gas Emissions and Buildings in the United Kingdom* (Watford: BRE, 1990).

M. Ridley, 'Acid rain – the risk to our stone buildings', *Estates Gazette*, **274** (29 June 1985), pp. 1320–2.

3 Site Hazards
Colin Ferguson

3.1 Introduction

With the rapidly growing interest in improving environmental performance in new buildings, it is sometimes easy to forget the inherent
environmental hazards posed by many development sites. The reality
is that, following large-scale industrial restructuring over the past 20
years, many industrial and commercial developments now take place
on or adjacent to land that was formerly put to contaminative use. In
some parts of the UK, and especially in SE England, the available
landbank is so small that sites are almost invariably redeveloped rather
than developed for the first time. In other areas, naturally occurring
pollutants such as radon can pose special problems for the developer.
On some sites, health hazards from the electromagnetic fields generated by overhead power lines may need to be considered. These are
the major issues addressed in this chapter.

Assessing the risks associated with site hazards is not easy; nor is
designing and constructing buildings that will provide adequate protection for subsequent users. Few of us can be expert, or even com-
petent, in all aspects of this work. For building professionals the key to
successful team working is understanding enough about the fundamental nature of problems to appreciate why other professionals
approach their job in the way that they do. Hence the emphasis in this
chapter is on understanding the issues, and appreciating the uncertainties, with a liberal supply of references to help the reader follow up
technical details.

3.2 Potentially contaminated land

Contaminated land is land which poses a hazard to human health or to
the environment, mostly as a direct result of past or present industrial
use. The scale of the problem is difficult to assess (see Table 3.1).

20

Table 3.1   *Estimates of potentially contaminated land in the UK.*

Source	Date	Region	No. of sites	Area affected (hectares)	Comments
DoE	1986	England	–	>10 000	Would be greater for the most sensitive uses (e.g. housing).
DoE[a]	1988	England	–	>26 000	40 500 ha of derelict land, 65% potentially contaminated.[b] Excludes land in use.
Welsh Office[c]	1988	Wales	746	>4000	Excludes small sites and land in use.
DoE[d]	1986/7	Cheshire	Ca. 2000	–	1577 sites identified with efficiency of 'more than 80%'.
ERL[e]	1990	UK	50 000 – 100 000	150 000[f]	No. of sites extrapolated from Cheshire survey.

[a] DoE, *Survey of Derelict Land in England 1988* (HMSO, 1991).
[b] House of Commons Paper 170-I, Vol. II, Ev. p. 3 (HMSO, 1990).
[c] Welsh Office, *Survey of Contaminated Land in Wales* (Welsh Office, 1988).
[d] DoE, *Pilot Survey of Potentially Contaminated Land in Cheshire – A Methodology for Identifying Potentially Contaminated Sites* (DoE, 1990).
[e] HC 170-I, Vol. II, Q891 (HMSO, 1990).
[f] Author's estimate assuming 75 000 sites with average area of 2 ha.

Section 143 of The Environmental Protection Act 1990 (see Section 9.3) places a duty on local authorities to compile and maintain public registers of land which may be contaminated. When these are open for public inspection a clearer idea of the extent of the problem should have emerged, at least for some contaminative uses.

Investigating potentially contaminated sites

A thorough environmental site investigation (ESI) is essential to avoid unnecessary risks to health and safety, costly unplanned remedial work during redevelopment or, in extreme cases, abandonment of the project. Developers and contractors also need to be aware that failure to conduct an adequate ESI could lead to prosecution under a wide variety of legislation [1]; in addition, the Control of Substances Hazardous to Health Regulations 1988 imposes new duties on employers in the construction industry [2], the Water Resources Act 1991 provides powers to the National Rivers Authority to enforce emergency clean-up of sites which threaten controlled waters, and the Environmental Protection Act 1990 strengthens previous provisions under the Public Health Acts relating to statutory nuisance. Finally, a developer could be exposed to civil liability for damage caused to the surrounding environment by migrating pollutants.

Fortunately, contamination is a material planning consideration so that, very often, the potential for contamination will be identified at the earliest stages of planning, and the necessary investigations carried out before the particular form of development is finalised.

The major aim of an ESI is to identify the hazardous substances present, their distribution over the site, and their concentrations at and below the surface. Guidance on the assessment of potentially contaminated land is provided by the Department of the Environment [3], the British Standards Institution [4] and the Institution of Environmental Health Officers [5]. A detailed and very useful account of the problems arising from the redevelopment of gas works and similar sites is also available [6].

Preliminary investigation

The initial phase of investigation of a potentially contaminated site should always include the following:

(a) A thorough review of site history and potentially contaminative uses.
(b) A review of the geology, hydrogeology and surface hydrology of the site and its surroundings, and of neighbouring land use.
(c) A site reconnaissance, wherever possible conducted after appraisal of the information compiled under (a) and (b).

The site reconnaissance is used to identify or confirm the positions of former structures (buildings, pits, lagoons, wells, underground storage tanks, etc), and to locate site hazards such as power cables, unsafe structures and contaminants visible at the surface. It thus serves the dual purpose of providing essential information for designing a cost-effective sampling plan, and assessing health and safety hazards. At the same time, some limited sampling at or near the surface (e.g. with a hand auger) can be undertaken.

Planning a detailed sampling programme

A poorly designed or too sparse sampling strategy may fail to identify critically contaminated areas and may thus lead to unacceptable health risks during or after development, or to expensive unplanned remedial work. Conversely, over-sampling is needlessly costly, and may still be ineffective. Official sources of guidance on sampling [3,4,7] lack detail and are inconsistent in their advice. The objective, clearly, is to use a sampling strategy that will maximise the probability (for a fixed cost) of identifying 'hot spots' where contaminant concentrations exceed critical values, or will minimise the cost for a fixed probability. New research to address this problem has been commissioned by the Department of the Environment [8].

Site investigation and assessment

An ESI needs to consider contamination of soils, surface water and groundwater, gas migration (see Section 3.3), and the protection of underground services and building materials. Expert knowledge is essential – a full account is beyond the scope of this chapter. The costs are site specific but can be considerable and include plant (excavators, drilling rigs, concrete breakers), chemical analysis of samples, and expert personnel. Safety should never be compromised and on some sites may involve appreciable additional costs for safety equipment, drench showers, clean areas for eating, etc.

The first objective of an ESI is to assess environmental hazards. Figure 3.1 shows that exposure to hazardous substances depends on a complex set of processes and migration pathways. It is important to remember that hazard refers to the potential to cause harm or damage, whereas risk is the probability that a hazard or hazards will result in specified harm to a specified receptor.

As the risks posed by contamination are difficult and potentially very costly to quantify, an indirect method based on 'trigger concentrations' has been devised in the UK [3]. Its purpose is to assist in selecting the most appropriate use for a site and in deciding whether remedial action is necessary. Tentative trigger concentrations have so far been set for only a limited range of contaminants, as shown in Table 3.2. In effect, two trigger values (a threshold level and an action level) define three zones as follows:

Zone A   All concentrations are below threshold trigger values; no remedial action is required and the site can be regarded as uncontaminated for the proposed end use.

Zone B   Some or all concentrations lie between the threshold and action trigger levels. There is a need to consider whether remedial action is justified for the proposed end use, or whether the end use should be changed.

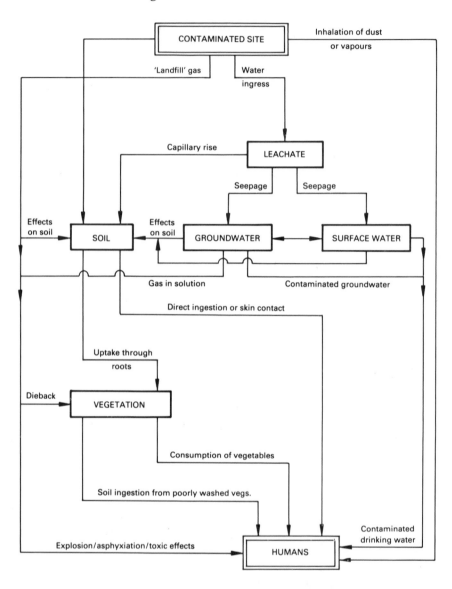

Figure 3.1   Schematic diagram showing contaminant migration pathways from a contaminated site to human receptors.

Zone C   Some or all concentrations are equal to or exceed the action level. Action of some kind, ranging from minor remedial work to changing completely the proposed end use, is unavoidable.

Table 3.2 *Tentative trigger concentrations for selected contaminants. Warning: this table is abridged and omits important conditions and footnotes without which the table cannot be used.*

Contaminant	A	B	C	D	E	F	G	Threshold	Action
								Trigger conc. (mg/kg air dried soil)	
Arsenic	•							10	NS
Arsenic			•					40	NS
Cadmium	•							3	NS
Cadmium			•					15	NS
Chromium (hexavalent)	•		•					25	NS
Chromium (total)	•							600	NS
Chromium (total)			•					1000	NS
Lead	•							500	NS
Lead			•					2000	NS
Mercury	•							1	NS
Mercury			•					20	NS
Selenium	•							3	NS
Selenium			•					6	NS
Polyaromatic hydrocarbons	•	•						50	500
Polyaromatic hydrocarbons				•	•	•		1000	10 000
Phenols	•							5	200
Phenols				•	•	•		5	1000
Free cyanide	•			•				25	500
Free cyanide					•	•		100	500
Complex cyanides	•							250	1000
Complex cyanides				•				250	5000
Complex cyanides					•	•		250	NL
Thiocyanate							•	50	NL
Sulphate	•			•				2000	10 000
Sulphate					•			2000	50 000
Sulphate						•		2000	NL
Sulphide							•	250	1000
Sulphur							•	5000	20 000

NS = not yet specified; NL = no limit – contaminant does not pose particular hazard for this use.
Key to planned uses: A: domestic gardens, allotments; B: play areas; C: parks, playing fields, open space; D: landscaped areas; E: buildings; F: hard cover; G: all proposed uses.

The current trigger value approach is incomplete, gives little guidance on appropriate responses for concentrations in Zone B, and makes no clear distinction between different types of exposure (ingestion, inhalation, skin contact) or between chronic (long term) and sub-chronic health effects. Nor is there guidance on interpreting the combined effects of multi-chemical exposures. The government is well aware of these deficiencies [9] and a research programme is underway to rectify them.

Remedial action

Remediation of contaminated soil and groundwater is a complex and difficult process. It demands awareness of many technologies (summarised in Figure 3.2) and their applicability and limitations, with sufficient depth of knowledge to appreciate the interplay between design, implementation, maintenance, monitoring and cost. By far the commonest remedial action in the UK to date has simply been to cap the contaminated area with hard cover (concrete or asphalt) or other impermeable material. However appropriate such action may be in some circumstances it is difficult to avoid the conclusion that capping is popular because it is cheap, cosmetic (out of sight, out of mind) and chosen because those responsible have little or no knowledge of alternative techniques.

Sadly, the UK lags far behind some other countries (e.g. Netherlands, Germany, USA) in site remediation. However, the Construction Industry Research and Information Association (CIRIA) has commissioned a major study to provide technical information and guidance on treatment methods and systems for the remediation of contaminated land. Publication is expected in 1993 and should do much to promote awareness of remedial technologies and their applicability.

Practitioners also need to be aware that remedial action can temporarily increase the contaminant loading to streams or groundwater; hence it is essential that the National Rivers Authority is fully consulted during design and implementation of remedial programmes. Similarly, site work can generate considerable quantities of hazardous dust, and sometimes harmful gases, into the atmosphere. Liaison with the local environmental health officer is essential.

3.3 Landfill gas

One of the effects of urban growth in post-1945 Britain is that many landfills, originally outside or on the fringes of urban areas, have now become prime locations for development. The pressure to redevelop on or adjacent to such sites is increasing, especially as this often provides an opportunity for restoring derelict land to beneficial use. For many older landfills little information may be available on the extent of the fill, its depth, or on the types of waste deposited. Earlier

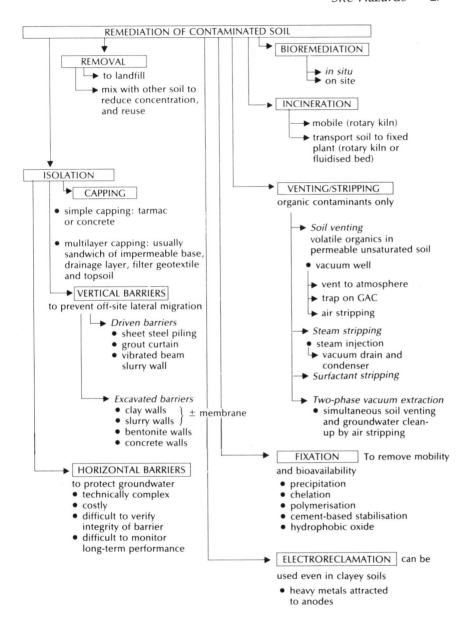

Figure 3.2 Summary of available technologies for remediation of contaminated sites.

comments on investigating contaminated land thus apply equally to landfill sites. The major difference is that the latter almost always pose additional problems relating to landfill gas [10].

Landfill gas is produced by the breakdown of biodegradable wastes, and typically comprises a mixture of methane (60–65 per cent) and carbon dioxide (35–40 per cent) plus trace concentrations of other gases. Methane is flammable at concentrations between about 5 and 15 per cent by volume in air. Without proper management the migration of gas from a landfill can pose risks of fire or explosion in nearby buildings, or of asphyxiation in confined spaces. These risks can continue long after a landfill ceases operation; the volume of gas emitted from old sites may be small but significant risks of explosive concentrations entering buildings can persist for several decades.

Landfill gas can migrate from a site through permeable strata, or for considerable distances along faults, fractures or fissures. It can pass along mine shafts and sewers or along the backfill around pipes and cableways (see Figure 3.3). It can also dissolve in leachate or groundwater, subsequently to be released some distance from the site boundary. Gas migration pathways can also be affected by changes in surface sealing caused by heavy rain, ice and snow, or by hard-cover development.

Building on or adjacent to landfill sites

After-use of landfill sites should normally be restricted to agriculture or, where permitted, conservation or recreational uses. On older landfills in urban areas, non-housing developments, such as retail or light industrial, may be appropriate but the difficulties of adequate site investigation and building design should not be underestimated. Planning authorities are required [11] to consult the relevant Waste Disposal Authority (WDA) on proposed developments within 250 metres of a landfill site, whether active or closed within the past 30 years. It is unlikely that a WDA will recommend housing development within 50 metres of any landfill unless rigorous monitoring [12] of the site has demonstrated that gas evolution has effectively ceased. For other developments a thorough site investigation will still be necessary. This will often reveal the need for protective measures which might include the following:

- Cut-off barriers or permeable venting trenches constructed between the landfill and the proposed development. Effective barriers can be difficult to install retrospectively around closed sites, and they should never be used as the sole means of control.
- Gas-proof barriers incorporated into the floor slab of buildings,

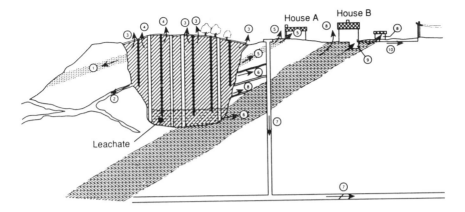

Gas pathways to atmosphere

① Through high permeability strata down the bedding plane

② Through caves/cavities

③ Through dessication cracks of the capping at the site perimeter, around tree roots, etc

④ Around site features which provide vertical pathways; gas or leachate wells

⑤ Through high permeability strata up the bedding plane, to atmosphere or house A

⑥ Through fissures caused by explosives, etc

⑦ Along man-made shafts, etc

⑧ Through highly fissured strata into the atmosphere or buildings such as house B or shed, etc

⑨ Into underground rooms

⑩ Along underground services

Figure 3.3 Possible landfill gas migration pathways from a completed/restored site. (Reproduced from reference 10 by permission of the controller of HMSO.)

with a high permeability layer beneath from which gas can be extracted [13]. Passive venting (see Figure 3.4A) is often favoured because it is maintenance free, except for ensuring that vent trenches and pipes do not become covered or choked. Such problems can be overcome by covering the vent trench (or doing without it) and inserting a vertical riser to vent the gas at roof level (see Figure 3.4B) using a rotating cowl or other suitable device to encourage flow. Fan-assisted ventilation, perhaps coupled to a gas detection and alarm system, may be appropriate for major developments where effective long-term maintenance can be ensured.

Regular monitoring of soil gas concentrations will need to be continued until it can be demonstrated that the gas source is effectively depleted. Developers need to be aware that it is their responsibility to ensure adequate monitoring to protect employees involved in the development and subsequent occupiers. If they fail to do so WDAs

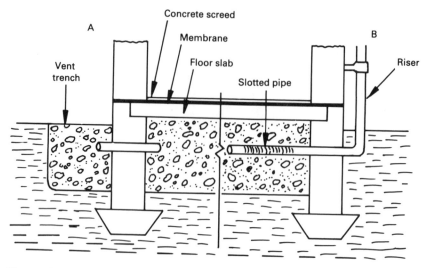

Figure 3.4   Basic methods for protecting a building from landfill gas using a gas-proof membrane and a ventilated layer beneath a floor slab.

have a duty [14] 'to do such works and take such other steps (whether on the land affected or on adjacent land) as appear . . . to be reasonable' to avoid pollution of the environment or harm to human health. They may also be entitled to recover the cost of doing so from the landowner.

It should be clear from the above that developing on or near a landfill site, whether active or closed, demands close consultation with the WDA and will usually require specialist technical help. It may also mean a long-term commitment to gas monitoring and maintenance of control measures, perhaps for several decades. To some extent these obligations and costs are the legacy of landfills that were poorly designed and managed, and inadequately regulated. Today the emphasis is on installing effective gas control measures at the outset and, increasingly, designing and operating landfill sites in such a way that their gas potential will be exhausted more rapidly. For the time being, though, building professionals need to recognise that special problems need special solutions. Fortunately, there is a growing body of expertise in academic institutions and commercial consultancies for tackling these problems.

3.4 Indoor radon and lung cancer

Indoor radon has been called the deadliest pollutant [15]. In the USA between 6000 and 24 000 lung cancer deaths each year have been

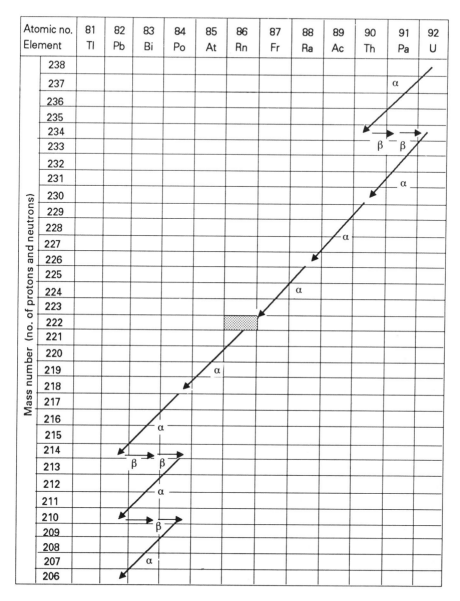

Figure 3.5   Simplified diagram showing the natural radioactive decay series from uranium-238, including radon-222 (shaded).

attributed to radon, with a best estimate [16] of 13 300 deaths. Radon is produced naturally from the radioactive decay of uranium and thorium in rocks [17]. Uranium occurs in crustal rocks at an average concentration of only 1 or 2 parts per million (ppm) but with higher levels in granitic rocks (about 4 ppm on average but with values of 10–20 ppm

Table 3.3   *Typical radioactivities from ^{238}U and ^{232}Th in rocks and building materials. Values relate only to parent radionuclide and thus exclude contributions from other members of the decay series.*

Material	Concentration (Bq/kg)	
	^{238}U	^{232}Th
Granite	90	80
Sandstone	20	10
Limestone	30	7
Cement	20	20
Sand and gravel	4	7
Clay bricks	50	45
Lightweight blocks	60	25

being by no means uncommon). Some shales and phosphate deposits also have relatively high uranium concentrations.

Understanding radon

Radon-222 is derived from the radioactive decay of uranium-238, as shown in Figure 3.5. Alpha (α) decay occurs when a nucleus spontaneously emits an α-particle, thus reducing the atomic number by 2 and the mass number by 4 (e.g. $^{238}_{92}U$ is transformed to $^{234}_{90}Th$). Beta (β) decay occurs when a neutron changes to a proton with emission of an electron, thus increasing the atomic number by 1 but leaving the mass number unchanged (e.g. $^{234}_{90}Th$ decays to $^{234}_{91}Pa$ and, by another β-decay, to $^{234}_{92}U$). A series of four α-decays and two β-decays transforms ^{238}U to radon ($^{222}_{86}Rn$) which in turn is eventually transformed to ^{206}Pb, a stable (non-radioactive) isotope of lead (see Figure 3.5).

Activity and dose

Radioactivity is measured in becquerels (Bq) in which 1 Bq is simply one radioactive disintegration per second. Typical activities of common rocks, and of building materials derived from rocks, are shown in Table 3.3.

   When radiation passes into biological tissue the energy absorbed per unit mass is called the absorbed dose; the unit of measurement is the gray (Gy) which is 1 joule of energy absorbed per kilogram of tissue. The energy released per atom in the decay steps from radon-222 to lead-206 is shown in Table 3.4. Note that much more energy is released by α-decays than by β-decays. But, because an α-particle has a

Table 3.4 *Breakdown characteristics of the steps from ^{222}Rn to ^{206}Pb in the ^{238}U decay series.*

Isotope	Half-life*	α-energy per atom (MeV)	β-energy per atom (MeV)	No. of atoms** in equilibrium with 3.7 Bq of Rn-222
Radon-222	3.82 days	5.48	–	
Polonium-218	3.05 min	6.00	–	977
Lead-214	26.8 min	–	0.62	8500
Bismuth-214	19.9 min	–	1.66	6310
Polonium-214	1.6×10^{-4} sec	7.68	–	0
Lead-210	22 years	–	0.02	
Bismuth-210	5.01 days	–	1.17	
Polonium-210	138.4 days	5.30	–	
Lead-206	Stable			

* Half-life is the time taken for half the atoms to decay to the daughter isotope.
** The number of atoms remaining after t seconds is given by $N(t) = N(0) \exp(-\ln(2)t/HL)$ where HL is the half-life in seconds. Thus after 1 second, 977 atoms of Po-218 will reduce to $N(1) = 977 \exp(-\ln(2)/183)$, which is 973.3 (hence 3.7 disintegrations per second, or 3.7 Bq).
Source: Data mostly from B. J. Wilson (ed.), *The Radiochemical Manual*, 2nd edition (Amersham: Radiochemical Centre, 1966).

mass more than 7000 times greater than that of a β-particle, its energy is absorbed within a very short distance – about 40 μm in tissue compared with several centimetres for a β-particle. Therefore, dose for dose, α-particles are much more damaging. To take this into account, radiation doses are usually expressed as dose equivalents measured in sieverts (Sv). One Sv is simply 1 Gy multiplied by a factor, Q, which is taken as 1 for β-radiation but 20 for α-radiation; that is, an absorbed dose of α-radiation is judged to be 20 times more damaging than a corresponding dose of β-radiation.

Why radon is the problem

Returning now to Figure 3.5, the isotopes from ^{238}U to ^{226}Ra are all solid metals and the radiation damage from their decay is largely contained within the rocks or building materials in which they occur. However, radon is an inert gas, which is virtually unable to enter into chemical reactions, and so it readily escapes from rocks and soils to enter the atmosphere [18]. Actually, the real culprits are the short-lived radon daughters, ^{218}Po, ^{214}Pb, ^{214}Bi and ^{214}Po. These are not gases but become attached to dust particles and, when inhaled, become lodged at various locations within the respiratory tract, depending mainly on the dust particle size. They can also form in the lung directly from radioactive decay of inhaled radon.

How much radon in indoor air?

Indoor air concentrations are mainly controlled by four 'P' factors:

- Production of radon, which primarily reflects underlying geology.
- Permeability of the soil [19].
- Perforations and other gaps in floors.
- Pressure differential between the air inside a building and that outside.

Average concentrations in Europe and North America (see Figure 3.6) mainly reflect differences in bedrock geology, type of soil cover, building practices and energy conservation measures (which sharply restrict ventilation and therefore promote radon accumulation). But these averages conceal huge variations. In the UK, for example, the average (about 20 Bq m^{-3}) conceals a range from almost zero to more than 2000 Bq m^{-3}.

Radon and lung cancer

The risks of developing lung cancer from radon daughter exposures have mostly been estimated from the study of exposed underground miners [20] in North America and Sweden. The literature is rather complex, not least because it uses a curious unit of radon exposure, the 'working level month' (WLM) [21]. But, roughly, 1 WLM corresponds to a dose equivalent in dwellings of 10 mSv, which is about the annual dose expected in a home with an indoor radon concentration of 200 Bq m^{-3}. And, even more roughly, lifetime exposure to radon daughters increases the lifetime risk of premature death from lung cancer by 0.25 per cent for each mSv annual dose [22]. Using these conversion factors, some UK and USA risks are summarised in Table 3.5.

It is estimated [16] that in the USA about 10 per cent of all lung cancer deaths may be due to indoor radon, this figure rising to about 14 per cent for residents in single-family dwellings. The excess risk for smokers (who are already at high risk) is much greater than that for non-smokers. Compared with the lifetime risk of dying in a road accident (about 1 in 140), the risks to the more exposed populations shown in Table 3.5 seem alarming. It should be remembered, how-

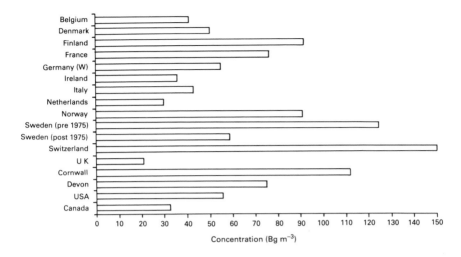

Figure 3.6   Mean or median indoor radon concentrations in Europe and North America.

Table 3.5   *Indoor radon concentrations, dose equivalents and approximate excess lifetime risk of lung cancer mortality for selected populations [22, 23, 24, 27].*

Population	Concentration $(Bq\ m^{-3})$	Dose equivalent $(mSv\ yr^{-1})$	Excess risk
UK average	20.5	1.02	1 in 390
USA average	55	2.75	1 in 145
Cornwall average	110	5.5	1 in 73
Cornwall (worst 5%)	>1000	>50	>1 in 8
Devon average	74	3.7	1 in 108
Avon average	42.1	2.1	1 in 190
SW England (worst 20%)	>400	>20	>1 in 20
Part of Northants*	>200	>10	>1 in 40

* Worst 25% of houses built on Northampton Sand Formation.
Note: National Radiological Protection Board action level for existing houses is 200 Bq m^{-3}.

ever, that the baseline average lifetime risk of lung cancer mortality is about 1 in 15. The average excess risk attributable to radon in the UK is therefore very low, although a causative link between radon exposure and other cancers cannot be ruled out [25]. Clearly, the need is to focus attention on high-risk areas such as Cornwall, to identify those buildings most at risk, and to provide effective mitigation measures for them.

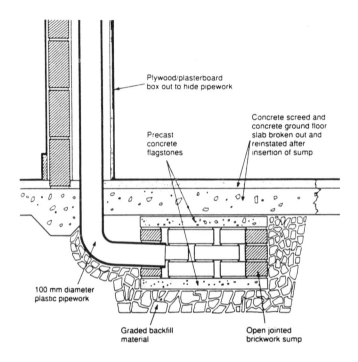

Plywood/plasterboard
box out to hide pipework

Concrete screed and
concrete ground floor
slab broken out and
reinstated after
insertion of sump

Precast
concrete
flagstones

100 mm diameter
plastic pipework

Graded backfill
material

Open jointed
brickwork sump

*Figure 3.7   Section showing construction of a radon sump.
(Reproduced from the article by Dixon and Gregory in* Building,
2 August 1991, p. 43 by permission of the editor.)

What can be done to reduce the risk?

The first priority is to identify areas and properties at risk through a
programme of long-term monitoring. Short-term measurements are
all but useless because ingress of radon depends on many time-
dependent factors such as ventilation performance, atmospheric
pressure, and wind speed and direction. A recent study [26] in Pennsyl-
vania showed that seasonal averages over a 2½-year period ranged
from 63 to 330 Bq m^{-3} while weekly averages ranged from 44 to
1140 Bq m^{-3}.

Most UK experience in reducing radon risks has been gained in
Cornwall using a range of techniques depending on the construction
of the building, its ventilation behaviour and the radon level. Construction of one or more radon sumps (see Figure 3.7) is the commonest technique and typically reduces the radon concentration by a
factor of 10 or more (see Table 3.6). For buildings with suspended

Table 3.6   *Reduction in radon levels in Cornwall using sumps.*

Building	Sumps	Ground floor area (m²)	Concentration (Bq m⁻³) Before	After	Reduction factor
College	1ª	500	1640	140	11.7
Medical centre	1	100	1290	70	18.4
School	3	200	730	80	9.1
School	4	450	970	120	8.1
Bungalow	1ᵇ	75	860	70	12.3
School	1	650	530	50	10.6
Offices	2	100	1150	150	7.7
School	5	500	770	70	11.0
Commercial	2	50	1480	90	16.4

ª Whole basement used as sump: two fans.
ᵇ External sump.
Source: D. Dixon and T. Gregory, 'Raid on radon', *Building* (2 August 1991), pp. 42–3, with permission of the editor.

floors, natural sub-floor ventilation can be increased using extra air bricks or larger grilles but radon reductions are rather small unless air flows are fan assisted. This technique may be used in conjunction with a membrane (1000 or 1200 gauge PVC) laid across the whole floor, fixed behind skirting boards, and sealed with mastic. But problems of dry rot have been encountered with timber floors due to increased moisture levels, thus raising doubts about the suitability of membrane barriers. For new dwellings, guidance on protective measures [28] is provided by the Building Research Establishment (BRE); again, it boils down to a combination of membrane barriers, underfloor ventilation or sump construction depending on the property. Improved techniques for radon mitigation are expected as experience grows and research results become available. Construction professionals should use the BRE's radon advice 'hot line' service for up-to-date guidance.

3.5 Overhead power lines

Of all site aspects perhaps the greatest uncertainty, and the fiercest controversy, is associated with the possible impacts of overhead power lines on human health. The problem first surfaced in the 1960s when reports from the Soviet Union [29] suggested that the extremely low-frequency electromagnetic fields (EMFs) created by overhead transmission lines (typically 50–60 Hz) might be responsible for a wide range of adverse health effects. These included headaches, depression, loss of appetite, adverse outcomes of pregnancy, disorientation and even suicide.

The evidence

It is one thing to report symptoms and short-term behavioural changes but quite another thing to conduct rigorous epidemiological [30] studies. The problem can be illustrated using a much quoted study [31] of 598 men and women in the West Midlands who committed suicide between 1967 and 1976. The same number of controls were chosen at random from the electoral register, and the authors claimed an association between suicide and residence close to overhead power lines. Others [32] dispute that the data support such an association. Nevertheless, in a later study [33] involving direct measurement of the 50-Hz magnetic field, it was shown that the suicide homes were exposed to a significantly higher magnetic field than the control homes. However, the controls were not matched with the cases for age, sex and social class and it remains quite possible that the suicides are wholly unrelated to magnetic field exposure. This demonstrates the difficulty of disentangling one factor from many other possible environmental or socioeconomic influences.

Recent studies have focused on magnetic fields (which, unlike electric fields, are not shielded by buildings) and their possible association with childhood cancer, especially leukaemia [34]. They suggest that children with high exposure to power line EMFs are about 1½ to 2 times more likely to develop leukaemia than children with low exposure. Surprisingly, though, this increased risk is apparent when exposure is estimated indirectly by 'wire coding' (i.e. according to the type of electric power lines near the home) but the relationship is much weaker or absent for directly measured EMF exposure. The explanation for this may be that wire coding is a better indicator of long-term field exposure than direct measurement; perhaps the latter fails to pick up aspects of EMF fields, such as infrequent but abrupt changes in field strength, which may be biologically relevant. But it could also mean that the cancers are caused by some other environmental factor that just happens to be correlated with wire coding. One possible factor that has been identified [35] is road traffic density with the implication of increased exposure to carcinogens such as benzene.

It needs to be emphasised that the studies referred to above do not imply a strong link between overhead transmission lines and adverse health. As yet there is no adequate explanation of how EMFs might initiate or promote cancer although mechanisms are being sought [36] and laboratory studies have demonstrated a wide range of biological effects [37] at relevant field strengths and frequencies. The problem is made even more complicated by exposure in the home to other EMF sources – electric blankets, hair driers, etc – and to higher frequency sources such as radar and microwaves [38]. Nor can we discount possible synergism [39] between combined exposure to chemical contaminants and magnetic fields.

The need for action

Given the confusing and inconclusive nature of the evidence, it is hardly surprising that those responsible for electricity transmission in Britain (National Grid Company and Scottish Power) maintain that the fields normally encountered in everyday life do not present health risks to the public. They take the view that, whereas it is proper for them to support epidemiological and other research, assessment of the evidence should be left to independent bodies; to date, these have provided no justification for changing current practice with regard to the routing of power lines and the siting of buildings close to them.

Pylons and power lines are ugly and can be noisy. Consequently, on aesthetic and amenity grounds, new lines tend to be routed away from properties wherever possible. Planning consent for buildings near existing power lines is controlled by local planning authorities subject to statutory clearance limits. The question remains – what weight (if any) should be assigned to possible health risks from overhead power lines? One view is that some conservatism in environmental risk assessment is necessary to protect the public (including those as yet unborn) from the adverse impacts of our own ignorance. The evidence for a small excess cancer risk, especially among children, may be insufficient [40] but it may still be prudent to mitigate that risk if we can. However, exposure depends both on field strength, which is a function of source magnitude and distance from source (see Figure 3.8), and exposure time. For any site within 100 metres of a high-voltage transmission line it may, therefore, be prudent to avoid any use, such as residential or school, involving long exposure times for children.

3.6 Summary

- Development sites may be contaminated by former industrial uses. Thorough site investigation is essential to avoid unnecessary risks to health and safety or costly unplanned remedial work. The aim is to identify hazardous substances present, their distribution, and their concentrations at and below the surface.
- A preliminary investigation should include a thorough review of site history, geology, hydrology and neighbouring land use. This review and a site reconnaissance are used to devise a detailed sampling plan.

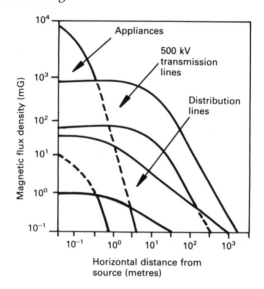

Figure 3.8   Variation in magnetic field exposure with distance from source.

- The main purpose of a full environmental site investigation is to assess environmental hazards and risks, and to judge whether remedial action is necessary for the proposed end use. There are many specialist technologies for remediation of contaminated soil and groundwater but, for some, little expertise and experience is available in the UK.
- Landfill gas is an additional problem on some sites and can give rise to fire, explosion and asphyxiation risks. It can migrate for considerable distances and may persist as a problem for decades after a landfill is completed. Special protective measures and rigorous long-term monitoring may be called for when developing on or near landfill sites.
- Radon, an inert gas derived from radioactive decay of uranium, can build up in poorly ventilated indoor spaces. When inhaled over long periods the daughter products of radon cause radiation damage to the lungs which can result in cancer.
- In the UK, indoor radon concentrations are highest in Cornwall where an active programme has identified areas and properties most at risk. Radon sumps, from which the gas can be safely vented to the atmosphere, have proved effective in reducing indoor radon concentrations. A membrane barrier can reduce radon ingress if carefully fitted but the most effective methods are underfloor ventilation and suction.
- Overhead power lines generate very low-frequency electromag-

netic fields which have been implicated in a range of adverse health effects. However, the evidence is far from clear and the issue is controversial. The evidence for a small excess risk of cancer (especially leukaemia) in children may be insufficient but, pending further research, it may still be prudent to avoid developments within 100 metres of high-voltage transmission lines that would result in long exposure times for children [41].

References

1. Summarised in Department of the Environment Circular 21/87 (Welsh Office 22/87), *Development of Contaminated Land* (London: HMSO, 1987). In Scotland *Planning Advice Note 33* should be consulted.
2. Construction Industry Advisory Committee, *The Control of Substances Hazardous to Health in the Construction Industry* (London: HMSO, 1989).
3. ICRCL 59/83, *Guidance on the Assessment and Redevelopment of Contaminated Land*, 2nd edition (London: Department of the Environment, 1987).
4. British Standards Institution, *Draft for Development: Code of Practice for the Identification of Potentially Contaminated Land and its Investigation, DD175* (London: BSI, 1988).
5. Institution of Environmental Health Officers, *Development of Contaminated Land: Professional Guidance* (London: IEHO, 1990).
6. Department of the Environment, *Problems Arising from the Redevelopment of Gas Works and Similar Sites*, 2nd edition (London: HMSO, 1987).
7. Department of the Environment (Standing Committee of Analysts), *The Sampling and Initial Preparation of Sewage and Waterworks' Sludges, Soils, Sediments, Plant Materials and Contaminated Wildlife Prior to Analysis*, 2nd edition (London: HMSO, 1986).
8. Preliminary results are discussed in C. C. Ferguson 'The statistical basis for spatial sampling of contaminated land', *Ground Engineering*, **25** (**S**) (1992), pp. 34–8. A final report will be published by HMSO in 1993.
9. Department of the Environment, *The Government's Response to the First Report from the House of Commons Select Committee on the Environment on Contaminated Land, Cm 1161* (London: HMSO, 1990).
10. Department of the Environment, *Waste Management Paper No. 27: Landfill Gas*, 2nd edition (London: HMSO, 1991).
11. The requirement is under the Town and Country Planning General

Development Order 1988 although this does not apply to Scotland.

12. Monitoring requirements are set out in Reference [10], paragraph 7.9.

13. Building Research Establishment, *Construction of New Buildings on Gas-Contaminated Land, Report BR 212* (Watford: BRE, 1991).

14. Under the Environmental Protection Act 1990, Section 61.

15. R. A. Kerr, 'Indoor radon: the deadliest pollutant', *Science*, **240** (1988), pp. 606–8.

16. J. H. Lubin and J. D. Boice, 'Estimating radon-induced lung cancer in the United States', *Health Physics*, **57** (1989), p. 417.

17. Only radon-222, derived from uranium-238, is considered in this chapter. Radon-220 (derived from thorium-232) and radon-219 (derived from uranium-235) also occur, but over 90 per cent of the radiation dose from indoor radon comes from radon-222.

18. Radon is soluble in water and so can also enter the body via drinking water although, for average exposures in the USA, this probably contributes only 1–3 per cent of the total dose equivalent. See T. A. Gosink *et al.*, 'Radon in the human body from drinking water', *Health Physics*, **59** (1990), pp. 919–24.

19. Clay has a relatively low gas permeability so that, if a house is built on boulder clay above granite, much of the radon emanating from the granite will decay to solid daughter products before reaching the atmosphere.

20. R. W. Hornung and T. J. Meinhardt, *Quantitative Risk Assessment of Lung Cancer in US Uranium Miners* (Cincinnati: National Institute for Occupational Safety and Health, 1987). G. R. Howe *et al.*, 'Lung cancer mortality (1950–1980) in relation to radon daughter exposure in a cohort of workers in the Eldorado Beaverlodge uranium mine', *J. Natl. Cancer Inst.*, **77** (1986), pp. 357–62. J. Muller, 'Study of mortality of Ontario miners, 1955–1957, part I', in H. Stocker (ed.), *Proc. Int. Conf. Occupational Radiation Safety in Mining* (Toronto: Canadian Nuclear Association, 1984). E. P. Radford and K. G. Renard, 'Lung cancer in Swedish iron miners exposed to low doses of radon daughters', *N. Eng. J. Med.*, **310** (1984), pp. 1485–94.

21. A 'working level' is defined as any combination of ^{218}Po, ^{214}Pb, ^{214}Bi and ^{214}Po in 1 litre of air that eventually results in the emission of 1.3 $\times$ 10^5 MeV of α-particle energy. This turns out to be approximately the amount of energy released by the four isotopes in equilibrium with 3.7 Bq of ^{222}Rn. Thus, from Table 3.4, we see that each atom of ^{218}Po, ^{214}Pb and ^{214}Bi eventually decays to ^{214}Po which, virtually instantaneously, releases 7.68 MeV of energy as it decays to ^{210}Pb. In addition, ^{218}Po releases a further 6.00 MeV per atom in decaying

to ^{214}Pb. Hence the total α-energy released is (977 + 8500 + 6310) × 7.68 + 977 × 6.0 = 1.27 × 10^5 ≈ 1.3 × 10^5 MeV. Exposure of a miner to this concentration for a working month of 170 hours (or to twice this concentration for half the time, etc) is a 'working level month', which thus reflects both concentration and exposure time.

22. J. I. Fabrikant, 'Radon and lung cancer: the BEIR IV report', *Health Physics*, **59** (1990), pp. 89–97.
23. National Radiological Protection Board, *Exposure to Radon Daughters in Dwellings*, NRPB G56 (Chilton: NRPB, 1987).
24. M. W. Courtis, 'The incidence of high radon concentration in United Kingdom domestic properties', *J. Radiol. Prot.*, **10** (1990), pp. 205–10.
25. D. L. Henshaw, J. P. Eatough and R. B. Richardson, 'Radon: a causative factor in the induction of myeloid leukaemia and other cancers in adults and children?', *Lancet*, **335** (1990), pp. 1008–12.
26. N. H. Harley and T. B. Terilli, 'Predicting annual average indoor ^{222}Rn concentration', *Health Physics*, **59** (1990), pp. 205–9.
27. D. S. Sutherland, 'Abstract: radon in Northamptonshire, England: geochemical investigation of some Jurassic sedimentary rocks', *Env. Geochem. Health*, **13** (1991), pp. 143–5.
28. Building Research Establishment, *Radon: Guidance on Protective Measures for New Dwellings* (Garston: BRE, 1991).
29. Reviewed in J. A. Bonnel, 'Effects of electric fields near power-transmission plant', *J. Roy. Soc. Med.*, **75** (1982), p. 933.
30. Epidemiology is the study of the distribution and determinants of disease in human populations.
31. M. Reichmanis, F. S. Perry, A. A. Marino and R. O. Becker, 'Relation between suicide and the electro-magnetic field of overhead power lines', *Physiol. Chem. Phys.*, **11** (1979), pp. 395–403.
32. See M. Coleman and V. Beral, 'A review of epidemiological studies of the health effects of living near or working with electricity generation and transmission equipment', *Int. J. Epid.*, **17** (1988), pp. 1–13. Also Bonnel, see Reference [29].
33. F. S. Perry, M. Reichmanis, A. A. Marino and R. O. Becker, 'Environmental power frequency – magnetic fields and suicide', *Health Physics*, **41** (1981), p. 267.
34. E. Wertheimer and E. Leeper, 'Electrical wiring configuration and childhood cancer', *Am. J. Epid.*, **109** (1979), pp. 273–84. D. A. Savitz, H. Wachtel, F. A. Barnes, E. M. John and J. G. Tvrdik, 'Case-control study of childhood cancer and exposure to 60 Hz magnetic fields?', *Am. J. Epid.*, **128** (1988), pp. 21–38. S. J. London *et al.*, 'Exposure to residential electric and magnetic fields and risk of childhood leukaemia', *Am. J. Epid.*, **134** (1991), pp. 923–37.

35. D. A. Savitz and L. Feingold, 'Association of childhood cancer with residential traffic density', *Scand. J. Work Environ. Health*, **15** (1989), pp. 360–3.

36. K. McLaughlan, 'Are environmental magnetic fields dangerous?', *Physics World* (January 1992), pp. 41–5.

37. I. Nair, G. Morgan and H. K. Florig, *Biological Effects of Power Frequency Electric and Magnetic Fields* (Washington, DC: Office of Technology Assessment, 1989).

38. K. R. Foster and W. F. Pickard, 'Microwaves: the risks of risk research', *Nature*, **330** (1987), pp. 531–2.

39. Synergism refers to the cooperative action of separate sources such that the total effect is greater than the sum of the effects of the sources acting independently.

40. National Radiological Protection Board, *Electromagnetic Fields and the Risk of Cancer*, DOCS, NRPB, Vol. 3, No. 1 (London: HMSO, 1992).

41. I am grateful to Mr Trevor Gregory, Professors Terry Lane and John Moohan, and Dr Tony Waltham for reviewing all or part of this chapter.

Further reading

D. J. Brenner, *Radon, Risk and Remedy* (New York: Freeman, 1989).

E. M. Bridges, *Surveying Derelict Land* (Oxford: Oxford University Press, 1987).

T. Cairney (ed.), *Contaminated Land: Problems and Solutions* (London: ESFN Spon, 1992).

4 Architecture and Landscape
Brian Carter

4.1 Introduction

Architecture establishes strategic decisions regarding the design of buildings and their relationship with and impact on the environment. Architects are responsible for preparing designs to satisfy the requirements of a client whether a home owner, an industrialist or a city father. However, the architect is also concerned with the relationships which a new building establishes with its surroundings, its detailed design, its construction and how it will perform in use.

In planning and designing a building for a particular setting, architects develop their ideas in collaboration with structural, mechanical, electrical and public health engineers, quantity surveyors, landscape architects and interior designers. It is important that this collaboration commences as early as possible, particularly in the design of large and complex buildings, and that it is maintained from the development of initial ideas through detailed design to the eventual construction of a building, for each of these disciplines has a major contribution to make. Thoughtful planning and an integrated approach to design can create buildings that are not only elegant but are also sensitive to their physical setting, economical to build, energy efficient, and which will have a long useful life.

There are a number of fundamentally important architectural issues that affect the environment both in and around a building which need to be considered in the development of any design.

4.2 Site planning

Each site for a building has unique physical characteristics as a result of its setting. This is equally true for both urban and rural sites where geology, altitude, landscaping and the surrounding landforms or buildings can significantly influence design. Such conditions can influence

45

the form and disposition of a new building. Isolated buildings in exposed conditions often need careful siting and planting to gain shelter from the wind and allow access to the sun, while larger traditional settlements consciously cluster to provide mutual shelter for both public and private spaces. Studies of the vernacular patterns of building can often highlight thoughtful considerations of site planning, micro-climatic factors and ingenious building design solutions.

This consideration of how site characteristics can influence the overall planning of a development through to the detailed design has influenced the work of the landscape architect Ian McHarg who has developed specific methodologies to ensure that the location and design of new developments is in harmony with the natural setting [1]. Also, schemes such as the project at Sea Ranch in California, which established a large new residential community on a particularly beautiful but exposed site overlooking the Pacific Ocean, have developed site planning strategies for the placement of development on the site and the shape of the new buildings which were directly influenced by studies of slope, landform and wind patterns over the site.

Within an overall site plan it is possible to influence the microclimate by design. For example, the use of water in courtyards and gardens will not only introduce calm but will also cool the surrounding spaces as a result of evaporation; again, new landscaping and planting planned as an integral part of building design can change the immediate environment by providing shade, ground cover or shelter belts for new development. The hedge shelters familiar in the western part of the Federal Republic of Germany are good examples of the traditional use of wind shelters (see Figure 4.1).

4.3 Orientation

The placement of a building on a site will significantly affect its quality, habitability and performance. There are obvious benefits which arise as a result of limiting glazed areas on exposed faces of buildings generally. Specific types of buildings may also work more satisfactorily with particular orientations. For example, in residential design it is desirable to plan living rooms with good sunlight and bedrooms which have morning sun. In designing offices where there is to be an extensive use of desktop computers it is advisable to provide a glare-free environment. This can be achieved by orienting glazed areas to the north. Alternatively, where glazing is directly exposed to the sun on south- or west-facing facades, screening significantly improves conditions for working. An example is shown in Figure 4.2.

In some climates, breezes are harnessed to improve living condi-

Figure 4.1 Traditional windshield hedges in northern Germany.

tions in buildings as is the case with the wind-towers which are incorporated into the design of some indigenous buildings of the Middle East in order to induce air movement.

4.4 The characteristics of materials

Careful consideration should be given in the specification of materials for new buildings. It is important to consider the energy consumption in manufacture and the durability of materials, as well as their safety in use. For example, timber, glass and steel are all materials which demonstrate a high structural strength per unit volume and consequently offer particularly unique economies in design. Similarly, building materials have different inherent characteristics and wherever possible it is helpful to make use of those characteristics in the design. A concrete floor slab, with its high thermal capacity, can retain heat and

Figure 4.2 (above and right)   Direct sunlight can strike the glazed walls of offices through a top-lit atrium and it is important to design internal screens which are appropriately located to protect work areas from glare and unnecessary heat gain. (Courtesy of Arup Associates, Architects & Engineers & Quantity Surveyors.)

re-radiate it back into a space – a characteristic which if utilised will tend to reduce the peaks and troughs of temperature normally experienced in a building and consequently tend to reduce the amount of environmental conditioning which will be required, as well as the long-term running costs of the building. The publication of BRE Current Paper 47/68 made it possible to calculate the thermal storage

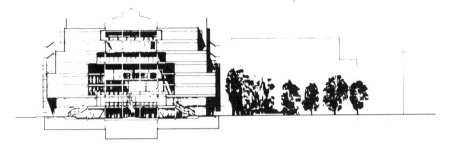

effects of building construction for the first time and some buildings, such as the SW Region Headquarters of the CEGB in Bristol, were designed to make specific use of this concept. In this particular project, cheap off-peak electricity was used to warm the large areas of concrete floor slab during winter nights with the heat re-radiated back into the space on the following day. In the summer the same slab was cooled during the evening in order to condition the space during the next day (see Figure 4.3). In some hot climates, however, buildings with a high thermal mass can create problems of overheating and a lightweight building envelope may be more appropriate.

The use of heavy structures can also improve acoustic performance. The offices for Penguin Books at Harmondsworth near to Heathrow Airport were designed with a double concrete roof structure with an air void in between the two leaves in order to provide high levels of acoustic insulation on a noisy site (see Figure 4.4).

4.5 The building envelope

It is important that the external envelope of a building is designed to provide an efficient wall-to-floor ratio as this will influence not only the initial cost of the building but also its performance over time with regard to maintenance, heat losses and cooling. The wall-to-floor ratio is aimed at maximising the amount of floor area contained by 1 m² of wall. Buildings which are long and thin in plan tend to have a high wall-to-floor ratio and consequently can be expensive to build and to operate. Square blocks are more efficient. A hypothetical 12-m square cube with a 3-m floor-to-floor height would have a wall-to-floor ratio of 1:1. In the design of offices, however, this standard is difficult to achieve and ratios of between 0.4:1 and 0.6:1 are more likely. The careful integration of architectural, structural and servicing systems can help to reduce floor-to-ceiling heights and consequently improve the ratio up to about 0.8:1 (see Figure 4.5).

In order to improve the efficiency of the building envelope, particularly in the design of office buildings, architects have developed the

Figure 4.3 (above and right)   At the offices for the SW Regional Headquarters of the CEGB in Bristol, the building fabric is used to assist cooling in summer. During the night, fresh air is passed through the hollow concrete floors thus cooling the structure. Daytime air passed through the same routes is then cooled by the concrete structure before it is distributed to the offices. When combined with reducing waste heat from lights and suitable shading of windows, it ensures that the office temperature can be maintained without the need for mechanical chilling. In winter, waste heat from machinery, lights and computers is stored in the staff swimming pool and is extracted by heat pumps for the hot water system. (Courtesy of Arup Associates, Architects & Engineers & Quantity Surveyors.)

concept of the atrium, first used in the Roman house (see Figure 4.6). Creating a covered space at the centre of a building improves the efficiency of the overall form by transforming external walls into internal partitions. In addition, the glazed atrium offers the potential to introduce daylight and outlook at the centre of a building as well as the opportunity to create through ventilation. By enclosing the space the heat gains and losses are reduced. An enclosed atrium also creates a

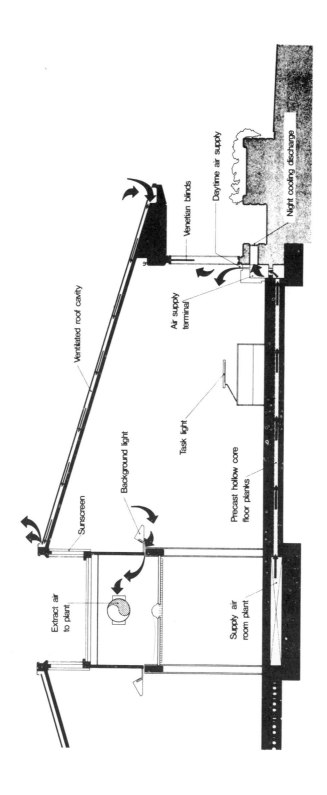

Ventilated roof cavity

Venetian blinds

Daytime air supply

Night cooling discharge

Air supply terminal

Background light

Sunscreen

Task light

Precast hollow core floor planks

Extract air to plant

Supply air room plant

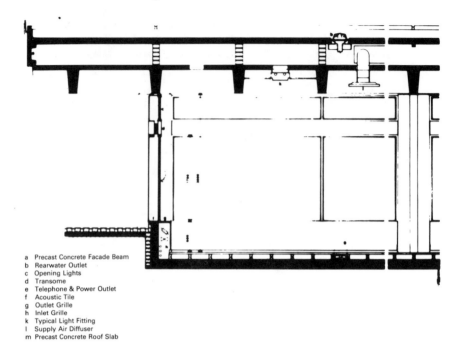

a Precast Concrete Facade Beam
b Rearwater Outlet
c Opening Lights
d Transome
e Telephone & Power Outlet
f Acoustic Tile
g Outlet Grille
h Inlet Grille
k Typical Light Fitting
l Supply Air Diffuser
m Precast Concrete Roof Slab

Figure 4.4   Diagram showing a roof construction designed to reduce air-borne noise from airplanes flying overhead. (Courtesy of Arup Associates, Architects & Engineers & Quantity Surveyors.)

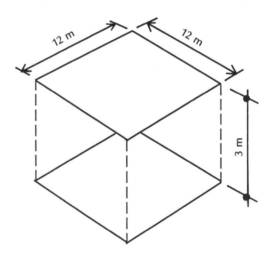

Figure 4.5   Diagram showing the basis of the wall-to-floor ratio.

generous day-lit space at the centre of a building which can be used for a wide range of amenities, such as restaurants, lounges and informal meeting areas. However, in planning these spaces special attention must be given to satisfying the regulations for protection in the case of fire.

The form of the building envelope can also be influenced by its setting. Developments on confined urban sites are frequently affected by requirements for daylighting, views and rights of light for adjoining properties, whilst urban design guidelines for new developments often establish massing envelopes, set backs and maximum heights for new buildings so as to retain particular views, respect the characteristics of an area or create new ones. In the countryside, similar constraints may affect the massing and form of the envelope of new buildings.

4.6 Building systems

Many systems are combined in the construction of a building. Systems of structure and the full range of building services including ventilation, electrical installations, water supply and drainage can usually be found in even the smallest building and the degree of complexity often increases with the size of the project. In a large modern building the building services can account for 40 per cent of the total cost of a project and consequently it is important to ensure that the design integrates all of these diverse systems in an economical and elegant manner. Although many of these systems are subject to change during the life of a building this change often occurs at different times. Building servicing systems are often replaced or changed more frequently than structural systems for instance. In some cases it is possible to establish likely degrees of change by examining how a particular building type works over time – this may influence the most appropriate strategy for the design. For example, office equipment may require relatively frequent changes of wiring whilst perhaps lighting or air conditioning may be changed less frequently. Designs should make provision for access and availability of space for those adjustments and changes to be made easily. This may also affect the design and selection of materials or furniture systems.

The structural system will tend to remain more static. However, as it often defines workspaces it is important for designers to test structural systems against different layouts. This is particularly relevant with regard to the depths of office spaces for space planning, access and daylighting to provide options for both open and cellular work spaces. Figure 4.7 shows the importance of good daylighting and efficient

Figure 4.6 (above and right)   Gateway 2 at Basingstoke is an office building with a floor area of about 16 000 m² where the offices are planned around a central atrium. The offices have views to the atrium as well as to the outside. As well as being an amenity the atrium also acts as a natural chimney drawing fresh air across the offices and out through opening ventilators in the roof. As a result, it is possible to ventilate naturally a building which would normally have required air conditioning. The occupants can control the degree of ventilation simply by opening or closing their office windows. By enclosing an internal courtyard, heat gains and losses are also reduced. (Courtesy of Arup Associates, Architects & Engineers & Quantity Surveyors.)

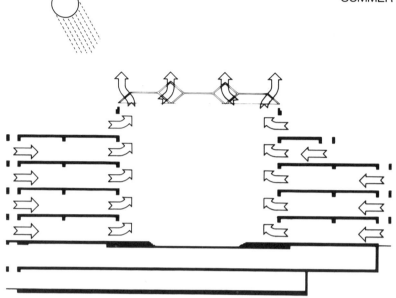

SUMMER

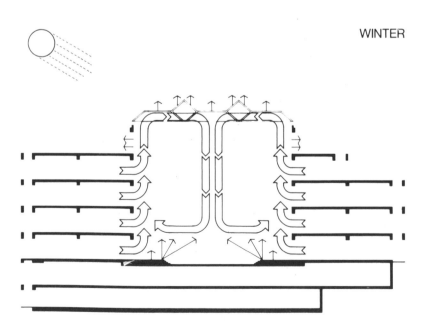

WINTER

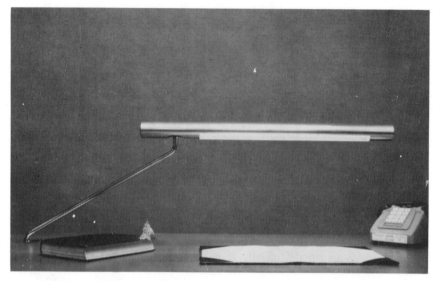

Figure 4.7 (above and right)   Buildings designed with good daylighting can save large quantities of energy. In designing artificial lighting systems, task lighting provides illumination directly on the workplace and uses less energy than ceiling lighting, whilst carefully designed uplighting provides reflected light without glare. A considerable proportion of a normal office air-conditioning load results from the waste heat created by lighting and the substantially reduced output from task lighting helps to reduce cooling loads. (Courtesy of Arup Associates, Architects & Engineers & Quantity Surveyors.)

artificial lighting. Office depths of between 15 and 18 metres glass to glass have tended to be the most widely used recently, with minor planning grids of 1.25, 1.5 or 1.8 m for office planning. These disciplines have tended to generate structural grids with spans of 6, 7.5 or 9 m, which are economical. In some offices the structure has been designed with longer spans in order to reduce the number of columns within work areas.

By careful design it may be possible to devise building systems which perform a number of different functions. If this is achieved then there are likely to be distinct cost benefits.

4.7 The design of the skin of the building

By careful design the external skin of a building can minimise heat losses. It can achieve this by providing high levels of insulation and can

also prevent excessive heat gain from solar penetration. The Building Regulations 1991 require that the external wall of an office building has a U value of 0.45 W/m²K. This can be achieved in a number of ways, including double-glazed opening windows and insulated spandrel panels. However, where possible, these standards should be improved upon in new buildings. For instance, the use of spandrels of masonry or high-performance glazing can significantly improve U values.

In contrast to a single-glazed window in a metal frame which would have a U value of 5.6 W/m²K, a double-glazed framed window with 'low-frequency' radiation heat-trap glass could provide a U value of 2.1 W/m²K. Although the initial cost of providing a high-performance external wall may be more expensive, it can provide cost benefits over the life of a building – the balance between the capital and operating costs should be examined during the development of the design. The roof of a building should also be considered carefully in the design of the external skin and its performance evaluated in a similar way to the walls. On flat roofs or terraces, external planting can provide valuable thermal capacity in addition to creating an amenity. A concrete roof structure with landscaping on top can provide a U value of around 0.23 W/m²K.

Whilst the design of the external skin itself can provide high levels of insulation it is also possible to improve its performance further by providing sun screening on exposed facades and highly glazed areas. If the sun does not penetrate the building then the radiant heat gain is drastically reduced. The most vulnerable facades for solar gain in buildings on sites in northern Europe are those facing south and west. Facades facing east are less susceptible to solar gain. However, there may be conditions on east-facing glazed facades where glare is a problem. The design of external screening should take into account the elevation of the sun which will be high in the sky on the south and require horizontal screens, whilst vertical screens are more appropriate to provide protection from the lower sun angles which are experienced on the east and west. It is possible to develop automated systems of external screening which are activated by strategically located sensors. Internal blinds can be used as an alternative form of screening with a greater degree of individual control. However, whilst they can be controlled easily by the occupants of a building these only offer protection from glare and not solar gain (see Figure 4.8).

The design of the window is an important part of the design of the external skin of most buildings, for it needs to provide good outlook with comfortable conditions without glare or draughts. In low-rise office buildings, as in residential developments, it may be possible to design windows for natural ventilation. In high-rise developments, special care must be taken to avoid excessive draughts, noise and discomfort.

4.8 Acoustics

Frequently, buildings are affected by noise. This may be air-borne noise resulting from the immediate surroundings, or structure-borne sound or noise which is caused by services such as air conditioning housed within the building envelope. Urban sites are often subjected to noise from surrounding roads, railways or aircraft. Care should be taken in the selection of sites so as to avoid aggressive noise climates wherever possible. However, where it is not possible to advise on site selection then particularly careful attention will be required in design to create good conditions within new buildings. Location and massing are important considerations. The greater the distance between a building and a noise source then the greater the reduction of the noise at the face of the building. If it is possible to shape the ground or construct barriers between the noise source and the building then this will improve conditions considerably. Substantial barriers of trees will help too, although not to the same degree as walls, mounds or other earthworks. The shape of the building can also help. For example, if a building is stepped with a series of terraces this can improve conditions (see Figure 4.9). If these terraces are landscaped then conditions may be improved even more. The detailed design can be developed too. Layered roof constructions create cavities which provide higher standards of acoustic protection from air-borne sound.

Structure-borne noise can be a problem within buildings, so planning studies should attempt wherever possible to zone noisy activities separately from more sensitive functions. In some cases it may be desirable to isolate structural systems to avoid the transference of noise. This is important in particularly sensitive types of buildings such as theatres, cinemas and recording studios. It is also an important issue which has to be carefully considered when designing air-rights buildings. For example, when offices are built over railway stations, new structural systems are sometimes mounted on isolating bearings to avoid the transference of sound.

Acoustic separation between offices may also be required for privacy and improved working conditions. Internal partitions should be designed to provide good acoustic insulation. Proprietary systems as well as specially fabricated installations can provide around 37 dB reductions between offices. The basic types are either single skin, double skin construction, double skin with a void or triple skin construction. Specialised systems can provide higher levels of insulation, provided that there are good connections at the head and sill. In offices where raised floors are used, care should be taken to avoid the transmission of sound via the floor void and the spaces above suspended ceilings.

If opening windows are required in an area where the noise climate is particularly aggressive then double or triple glazed units may be

Figure 4.8 (above and right)   External sun shading can prevent the sun penetrating into a building and thereby drastically reduce the radiant heat gain. By careful design it should protect the interior from summer sunshine while ensuring good outlook for people using the building. (Courtesy of Arup Associates, Architects & Engineers & Quantity Surveyors.)

considered. Ventilation slots should be designed with attenuation to prevent the direct entry of sound and consideration should be given to the design and dimension of the cavity between the leaves of glazing. A window with a 500-mm wide cavity between inner and outer panes and acoustic reveals within the cavity (and where there is no direct acoustic path when such a window is open) can achieve a facade insulation performance of 15 dB(A).

4.9 Performance

Design ideas may be relatively easy to come by. However, it is important to check and assess their validity in practice in order to ascertain their appropriateness. Many different aspects of a building can be monitored in use. For example, one study of temperatures within an office building planned around a central atrium was conducted over a 12-month period in order to ascertain if the use of atria to encourage cross-ventilation worked satisfactorily and induced natural ventilation as predicted in the design proposals [2]. Other studies have examined the performance of specially designed external wall constructions, mechanical systems and lighting design.

At Briarcliff House in Farnborough the office environment was surveyed over a year. As a part of this study the external skin of the building, which consisted of a double glass wall with a 600-mm air gap

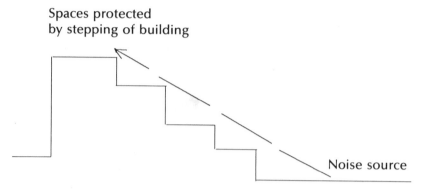

Spaces protected
by stepping of building

Noise source

*Figure 4.9   Diagram of building with stepped profile to reduce
air-borne noise.*

between, was examined in use over a year. The external and solar wall gap temperatures were measured each hour in order to establish the precise amount of the heating load for the ventilation air that was provided by the solar preheating of air drawn from the glazed wall. In addition, the double skin improved the U value from the normal 5.6 W/m²K for single glazing to approximately 3.0 W/m²K, realising a saving on the heating load and creating an estimated total saving in the primary energy consumption of 3 per cent compared with a conventional air-conditioned office [3]. Such studies of how buildings perform in practice are invaluable for design innovation, but they require the commitment of both the designers and the client (see Figure 4.10).

Tests of components are also important in the design and construction of a building. These tests may be carried out by manufacturers, but can also be commissioned either by designers or their clients from independent testing authorities.

There are a variety of ways of assessing the environmental performance of buildings, including BREEAM by the Building Research Establishment. The impact of buildings should be assessed both at the design stage and during use. Chapter 10, on environmental assessment, sets out the ways in which this can be achieved.

Life cycle costing is a technique which has been developed to add a financial dimension to design decisions. It allows comparisons to be made at the design stage in order to examine the merits of investing in the most appropriate option. The technique cannot be used by the design team in isolation and it is necessary to work in close conjunction with the client and his financial and legal advisers. Considering life cycle implications in terms of design as a separate area from low energy cost and low maintenance cost is a way of seeking to achieve a long building life with the minimisation of maintenance operations.

This will tend to reduce disruption of the use of the building, as well as damage to the fabric, in carrying out repair work. Ultimately, one is seeking value for money spent in terms of performance gained over the life of the building. This matter is also dealt with in Section 5.12 of Chapter 5, on energy efficiency.

4.10 Summary

- Ensure that the design of a new building is developed by the architect, working in close consultation with all of the other design disciplines, from the conceptual stages through detailed design and construction.
- Consider the siting of a new building with particular attention to the natural characteristics of the site to make every effort to build on reasonably flat, dry land and avoid steeply sloping sites, flood plains and high-quality agricultural land.
- Orientate new buildings to create outdoor and indoor spaces which will benefit from sun, views and shelter from the wind.
- Design clearly articulated systems of structure and environmental servicing and ensure that they are carefully coordinated and integrated together.
- Consider the palette of materials from which a building will be constructed for its appropriateness with regard to surroundings, performance and long life.
- Examine the design of the external skin of the building with reference to both its aesthetic qualities and its function. Ensure that it is highly insulated and that glazed areas are designed to provide good levels of daylighting internally, but avoid excessive solar gain and glare.
- Investigate the opportunities to specify materials which have low primary energy consumption, yet have a long life.
- Test and evaluate the environmental systems of new buildings in design and monitor them wherever possible once in use.

References

1. Ian L. McHarg, *Design with Nature* (New York: Doubleday/Natural History Press, 1971).
2. *Data Build* (1991).
3. *Project Monitor*, Commission of the European Communities, Issue 12, December 1987.

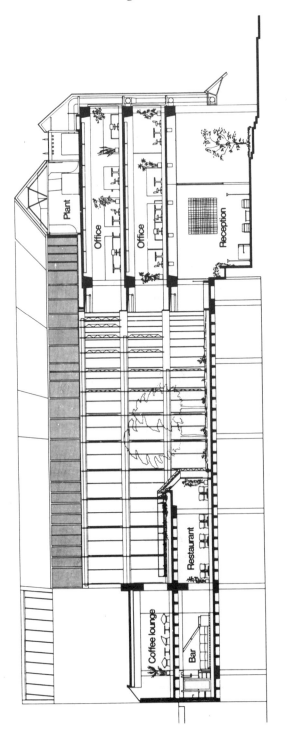

Figure 4.10 (above and right)   The southern elevation of Briarcliff House is designed as a double skin which has been specially designed to exclude solar gain and traffic noise from offices on an urban site in Farnborough. The outer leaf, which is totally glazed with bronze tinted glass, acts as a flysheet which shields the building from the weather and provides a consistency of appearance, while the inner leaf which is part of the office layout is made up of solid and glazed panels which can be arranged to suit changing needs. Heat in the space between the two leaves is controlled so that it may be used to help heat the building in winter. In summer, exhaust dampers at high level enable the natural convection between the two leaves to help keep the building cool. (Courtesy of Arup Associates, Architects & Engineers & Quantity Surveyors.)

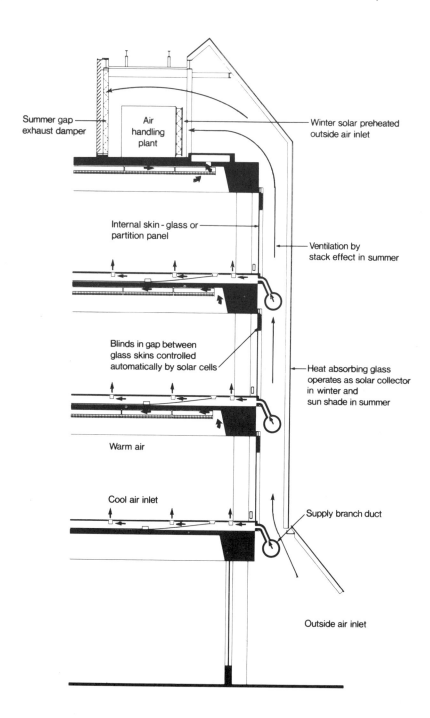

Summer gap exhaust damper

Air handling plant

Winter solar preheated outside air inlet

Internal skin - glass or partition panel

Ventilation by stack effect in summer

Blinds in gap between glass skins controlled automatically by solar cells

Heat absorbing glass operates as solar collector in winter and sun shade in summer

Warm air

Cool air inlet

Supply branch duct

Outside air inlet

Further reading

Bruce Anderson (ed.), *Solar Building Architecture* (Massachusetts: MIT Press, 1990).

R. Banham, *The Architecture of the Well-tempered Environment* (London: The Architectural Press, 1969).

B. Carter, 'Coming to terms with climate', *The Architectural Review* (June 1991).

CIBSE Guide – Volumes A, B, C (London: Chartered Institution of Building Services Engineers, 1988 and updates).

Davis and Ventre (eds), *Performance of Buildings and Serviceability of Facilities* (USA: ASTM, 1990).

Friends of the Earth, *Good Wood Manual & The Good Wood Guide* (London: Friends of the Earth, 1990).

Randall McMullan, *Noise Control in Buildings* (London: BSP Professional Books, 1991).

P. H. Parkin, H. R. Humphreys and J. R. Cowell, *Acoustic Noise and Buildings*, 4th edition (London: Faber Paperbacks, 1979).

D. Patterson, *Commercial Timbers of the World* (Aldershot: Gower Publishing, 1988).

N. Pevsner, *A History of Building Types* (London: Thames & Hudson, 1976).

5 Energy Efficiency
Stuart Johnson and Andrew Wilkes

5.1 Introduction

The government energy-saving campaign 'Helping the Earth Begins at Home' launched in Autumn 1991 stated that domestic fuel bills could be cut by 20 per cent or more by straightforward changes such as improved insulation and draught-proofing. The campaign stresses the need to reduce carbon dioxide emissions as well as pointing out the possibility of lower bills. This action is an advance of an international agreement on the use of fossil fuels and global warming which is expected to be signed in 1992. Given that demand for electricity is increasing world-wide, particularly in less developed countries, it is possible that the UK and other developed nations will have to reduce consumption of fossil fuels by about 50 per cent over the course of the next thirty to thirty-five years. Reductions in energy consumption of this order are feasible and after the initial pay-back period, saving would have an appreciable affect on individuals' living standards and companys' profitability [1]. If there is one theme underlying the increased awareness about environmental issues, it is that our squandering of energy and other resources must end.

A detailed account of the environmental arguments is given in Chapter 2, on environmental issues, but they are repeated in broad terms here. The gases emitted when fossil fuels are burnt for electricity generation contribute towards global warming and acid rain. As about a half of all the gases responsible for global warming are carbon dioxide, and around 50 per cent of all carbon dioxide emitted is directly related to space heating and cooling, water heating and lighting, our use of buildings has a major environmental dimension [2]. The gases responsible for acid rain include sulphur dioxide, nitrogen oxides and hydrocarbons and, in Britain, sulphur dioxide is the most significant contributor. Most sulphur dioxide emissions arise from burning fossil fuels in power stations and this strengthens the environmental argument for maximising energy efficiency of all of our buildings.

Both the insulation standard of building fabric and the performance of services influence energy efficiency of property. This chapter examines ways of improving efficiency at the design stage and during the life of the building, together with the relationship between capital and running costs. Chapter 4, on architecture and landscape, should be referred to for advice on building orientation and landscaping as examples of ways in which building design can influence energy use.

5.2 Benefits

The Gulf crisis once again threw our reliance on oil in the developed world into sharp relief. Our use of non-renewable energy resources such as oil is beginning to change as its cost increases in real terms, particularly when oil supplies are disrupted. Also, there are the environmental issues and this was acknowledged in the government's recent White Paper on the environment which stated that 'energy efficiency improvements are the cheapest and quickest way of combating the threat of global warming' [3]. These issues can only adopt increasing prominence as time goes on. This is not to say that a greater proportion of our electricity will not be generated without the use of fossil fuels in the medium to long term. However, this is outside our direct control so, in the meantime, we should take individual responsibility for energy conservation.

Energy is now a significant proportion of total occupation costs for most buildings, but it is a myth that efficiency methods are rarely cost effective. This has been recognised in Milton Keynes where all new buildings must meet high standards of energy efficiency. It is estimated that this adds about 1 per cent to construction costs, but reduces energy consumption by about 40 per cent [4]. Cost control, whilst undoubtedly important, is only part of the equation; the effect on property values is just as significant. As energy costs are usually borne by building occupants, many developers, landlords and their advisors have traditionally expressed little interest in energy efficiency. This is a short-sighted approach, as occupants give a high priority not only to the rent but to a building's total running costs and therefore buildings which can demonstrate lower energy consumption than other similar buildings will be more desirable. This can often justify higher rents and thereby higher capital values.

There is real and increasing concern about the environment and many players in the property and construction markets are beginning to formulate environmental policies. It does not take a great stretch of the imagination to forecast that properties which are perceived to be environmentally unfriendly will show a decrease in value in real terms in the future. Now is an ideal opportunity for everyone involved with property to maximise the energy efficiency of buildings, either for financial or environmental reasons.

Evermore regulation and legislation is affecting energy performance of buildings, and it will surely not be too long before greater energy conservation is no longer discretionary. For a number of reasons, taxation to increase the cost of fossil fuels is becoming an increasingly attractive option for the government. The forthcoming international agreement on carbon dioxide emissions mentioned earlier in this chapter may ultimately give rise to the need for such legislation, but another reason might be to reduce our reliance on oil imports from less reliable sources. Even if legislation does not come directly from the British government, it may come from the EC who are contemplating an energy or carbon tax [5]. Chapter 9, on environmental law, sets out the current position of energy efficiency and the law.

5.3 Thermal insulation

Improved insulation of the building fabric is probably the most obvious and cost-effective form of energy conservation. However, it cannot be considered separately from the other aspects of energy efficiency such as performance of the services plant. According to the Energy Efficiency Office 'many well-insulated offices have higher heating costs than predicted because the plant cannot cope efficiently with low heating loads or make effective use of "free" heat gain. The result is often over heating (with further heat loss from the window-opening) and poor plant efficiency' [6].

The starting point for determining the level of insulation for new buildings is the Building Regulations 1991. Part L of these regulations deals with conservation of fuel and states that reasonable provision shall be made for the conservation of fuel and power in buildings [7]. There is discretion on how this provision can be achieved, although Part L (Approved Document) does suggest some ways of meeting it in respect of insulation of the building fabric, boiler controls, and insulation of hot-water storage vessels, pipes and so on. This section deals only with insulation of the building fabric where Part L offers two approaches: elemental and calculation. If an elemental approach is adopted, the levels of insulation shown in Table 5.1 are to be achieved for specific building elements.

The figures referred to in the building regulations are known as U values and are a measure of the thermal insulation offered. Obviously, not all building materials offer the same degree of thermal insulation and to meet building regulation standards it is necessary to incorporate

Table 5.1 *Levels of insulation to be achieved for specific building elements.*

Building element	Housing	Non-housing
Walls, floors and ground floors	0.45	0.45
Roofs	0.25	0.45
Semi-exposed walls and floors	0.6	0.6

All figures are measured in W/m²K.

materials with a high degree of thermal insulation, such as mineral fibre quilts, in addition to the materials required as part of the structure or weatherproof envelope. Part L allows U values to be increased (that is, the level of thermal insulation to be reduced) if windows are double glazed or more insulation is provided to the ground floor slab. The Approved Document L1 offers guidance in how U values can be estimated for the proposed construction of different elements of the building and thereby allows the thickness of insulation material required to be determined. There is a procedure for calculating U values in Appendix A or the tables in Appendix B can be used. If the elemental approach is adopted, the area of single-glazed windows and rooflights must be kept within particular limits. For example, in office buildings, windows must not exceed 35 per cent of the exposed wall area. There are different limits for other building types, but all of the maximum areas can be increased if double, triple or low emissivity coated glass is used. Where the elemental procedure is inappropriate, Part L (Approved Document) offers two calculation approaches which give greater flexibility in design to meet energy targets.

Many people who are concerned about the environment have criticised the U values contained within the building regulations as being inadequate. The standards have been increased periodically and this process is likely to continue in response to concern about the environment and consumption of energy. Comparison with thermal insulation standards elsewhere in Europe is interesting. Eurima, the European Insulation Manufacturers' Association, has recently produced a report entitled 'Thermal insulation standards in housing in Europe' [8]. Figure 5.1 is abstracted from their report and shows insulation thicknesses required to satisfy insulation standards for both roofs and walls in 15 different countries. It can be seen that, in general terms, greater insulation is demanded in northern Europe but this generalisation conceals many exceptions. The Energy Directorate of the European Commission is at an early stage in its consideration of a proposed directive of pan-European insulation standards. It is likely that any

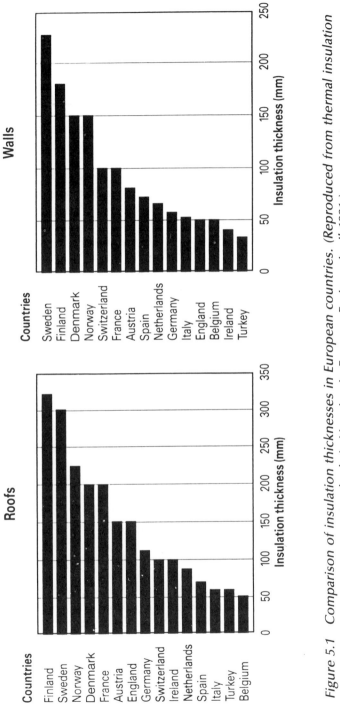

Figure 5.1   *Comparison of insulation thicknesses in European countries. (Reproduced from thermal insulation standards in* Housing in Europe, Eurima, April 1991.)

directive will acknowledge climatic and energy cost variations across the community in establishing insulation standards. The trend across Europe is for increasingly high levels of thermal insulation – even if this does not come directly from Westminster, it may well come from Brussels.

It is difficult to give guidance on the degree of insulation that should be achieved for individual buildings, although certainly the current building regulations should be met. There is scope for considerably greater levels of thermal insulation, although care must be taken that the energy consumed in producing and transporting the insulation material is not greater than the energy saved. Eurisol, the UK mineral wool association, has done some useful research in this area and identifies the concept of an 'environmental thickness' of insulation. Given certain assumptions which will vary from building to building, the level of insulation where more energy is consumed in its production than is ever saved is far greater than the practical insulation thickness. They suggest that mineral wool insulation batts would have to be 700 mm thick for cavity walls before overall energy efficiency begins to decrease [9]. Each building should be considered separately. Issues to be addressed include the objectives of those with an interest in the building, the relative importance of capital and running costs, and construction matters. The checklist set out below is a useful tool in determining the degree of insulation to be achieved for a specific new building.

Checklist to determine the degree of thermal insulation

- Does environmental concern outweigh strictly financial considerations?
- What is the relative importance of capital versus running costs?
- What pay-back period (or discounting rate) applies if thermal insulation is to be greater than current building regulation standards?
- Does the enhancement of building value arising from high levels of insulation need to be taken into account?
- Is the building heated and occupied regularly in order to make high levels of thermal insulation worthwhile?
- Can the construction method and materials proposed accommodate enhanced thermal insulation?
- Do the proposed construction method and materials offer appropriate durability?
- Do the proposed construction methods and materials lend themselves to current expertise and standard of workmanship likely to be encountered on site?

This checklist may well require modification to suit individual circumstances. Of the considerations identified in the checklist, one of particular concern is whether non-traditional construction and materials will prove durable. Attention should be given to the implications of filling cavities with insulation and detailing around windows and other openings to minimise the risk of water penetration to the inner leaf of cavity walling. Other implications to be aware of are cold bridging, allowing condensation internally, and interstitial condensation where inadequate vapour checks or ventilation can allow condensation within a building element, such as a wall or roof. Nevertheless, there are many practical ways in which thermal insulation standards can be enhanced without compromising durability or weathertightness.

Building regulations apply only to new construction and because new buildings account for only a tiny proportion of the total property stock, many of our buildings are either un-insulated or insulated to a very poor standard. In order to make a meaningful reduction in the pollution arising from our use of buildings, every effort must be taken to improve their energy efficiency and this includes enhanced levels of thermal insulation. Obviously, it can be more expensive and disruptive to add insulation to an existing building than a new one, but this can be minimised if the work is carried out at the time of refurbishment, maintenance or redecoration. The debate about the standard of thermal insulation to be adopted is much the same as for new buildings, with building regulations providing a starting point.

5.4 Local materials

Commitment to energy conservation demands local sourcing wherever possible, to minimise the energy consumption when transporting the materials to site. A conscious decision is required due to the imperfections of the market, where materials which have been transported over long distances are not necessarily more expensive than local equivalents. Such a commitment does not limit choice unduly as Britain is well served with supplies of construction materials. It is accepted that local sourcing is not always possible and NEDO acknowledges that it is difficult to procure British curtain walling systems. They report that 'Lloyds is a most British Institution; its new building is 75% British. Unfortunately its external appearance is entirely dependent upon imports because Britain could not supply the products in time nor at the right price. This story is repeated at Broadgate and again at Heathrow, where the first building international visitors see is Terminal 4, clad in West German stainless steel' [10]. However, the principal concern is with transport of bulky, low-value products over long distances such as cement, aggregate and stone.

5.5 'Hidden' energy costs

The manufacture of building materials entails energy consumption and this varies widely depending on the product, but will not necessarily be reflected in the price. By way of example, steel and cement use a large amount of energy in production whereas timber does not. A specific example is that of mineral wool production which uses about 10 per cent of that consumed by expanded polystyrene [11]. This is an example of energy consumed during the manufacture of thermal insulation and it is possible to conceive that this may be greater than the energy that is ever saved during a building's life, especially with infrequently heated, short-life properties. It is unfortunate that insufficient research has been undertaken into the energy consumed during the manufacture of building materials to allow choices to be made with a great degree of confidence. Over time, this information will become available. In the meantime, a useful rule of thumb is that the greater the degree of processing or manufacture, the greater the energy consumed.

5.6 Design life of buildings

Buildings with a long life expectancy imply energy efficiency because they make good use of building materials by minimising the impact of manufacture, processing, transport and installation. The design life of a building has two components, durability and flexibility, which combine to avoid premature failure and obsolescence.

Traditionally, British buildings have been designed with a life expectancy in excess of 60 years which makes good use of building materials, many of which are from finite resources. However, there is a trend towards adopting materials and techniques which will give rise to a shorter life expectancy, for example lightweight profiled metal cladding systems which are commonly used on industrial and warehousing buildings. To minimise environmental impact, durable and soundly detailed individual elements should combine with ease of maintenance to create a building of maximum life expectancy. This is not to say that financial considerations should be ignored, but a building which will remain sound in the long term is not incompatible with maintaining value in real terms. Consideration of these issues is not carried out as a matter of course, even on landmark buildings costing tens of millions of pounds. With a new development, the brief should demand the preparation of a schedule indicating the life expectancy of major building elements, together with their ease of maintenance.

A durable building is of little benefit if it has built-in obsolescence.

Thus, it is important that all buildings are as flexible as possible so that they can accommodate the changing needs of occupiers. Factors maximising flexibility depend upon the type of building, but areas worthy of consideration typically include floor-to-ceiling or eaves height, good day lighting, adequate provision for horizontal and vertical distribution of services, reasonable permissible imposed loadings of the floor slabs and minimal structure away from the perimeter which allows flexibility of layout.

5.7 Out-of-town schemes

Many out-of-town business parks, industrial estates and retail schemes are built with high levels of thermal insulation and efficient services plant. Nevertheless, because of the fuel used in transporting building users from their homes, the whole scheme may be very inefficient in energy terms. Vehicles are a significant contributor towards global warming and acid rain, but unfortunately there is little information available on the relationship between out-of-town developments and these phenomena.

An increasing desire for total energy efficiency combined with an ageing population because of demographic trends may lead to the resurgence of the town centre in the long term. Most non-town centre sites are selected because of their proximity to roads and are often poorly served by public transport. A way of mitigating the energy consumed by transport is car sharing or perhaps a bus linking with existing public transport services; owners and occupiers of out-of-town schemes can organise this.

5.8 Energy savings in building systems and services

There are many factors affecting the current impetus, or perhaps it should be lack of impetus, in maintaining a positive approach towards energy savings relating to mechanical and electrical (M&E) systems and services within buildings. The current situation is completely different than in 1974 when inefficient systems and structural envelopes gave greater scope for reduction in energy demand. Since then the energy-using countries have addressed the fundamental issues of inefficiency (at least for new buildings) although the primary emphasis has been at a micro- rather than the macro-economic level.

Until the 1960s the primary reason for energy usage within buildings in the UK and northern countries of Europe was due to lighting and heating. Rapid increases in the creation of wholly artificial, air-conditioned buildings brought about a vast increase in energy usage. Unfortunately, this type of building has been, until very recently, perceived as 'high quality' or luxurious, giving rise to a high demand for this type of highly serviced space. In the UK especially, property developers found air-conditioned buildings tended to let more quickly and they proliferated.

During the past decade an upsurge in information technology (IT) equipment use has spread throughout the office rather than in confined areas such as computer suites. What has resulted is the perceived need to maintain a 'luxury product' with air conditioning but with the penalty of ever-increasing energy use. Building running costs are always difficult to predict, so the promise of lower operating costs and energy-saving measures has been frequently ignored by even the most prudent and circumspect of owners or occupiers.

One of the difficulties facing any owner of a new building is interpretation of advice relating to the future investment potential of the completed structure. The perceived 'quality' of the product and the flexibility of the space to accommodate any type of user has resulted in more and more buildings following the fully air-conditioned route often with deep-plan floorplates, non-opening windows and floor-to-ceiling heights that are so shallow that proper air movement or temperature migration from anything other than the mechanical HVAC (heating/ventilating/air-conditioning) systems is restricted. The trend towards 'isolating' the internal environment from the external influences has similarly created higher, rather than lower, energy demand because of the artificial lighting provision to counteract the lower fenestration ratios and the larger air-conditioning plant.

The undoubted advantages of office system technology have brought with them increased demands for accommodation and energy loads. The much misunderstood loadings of such equipment is exacerbated by the inevitable 'crystal-ball' gazing when endeavouring to ensure that the M&E systems and services are provided to keep pace with IT proliferation. The heat output of a typical desktop computer with a colour VDU screen is approximately 350 W while that of a laser printer is 450 W. Assuming an occupation density of 1 person per 8 m^2 this equates to a typical equipment gain of 100 Wm^2. In order to maintain the flexibility demanded by the brief for the building, it is often extrapolated that the heat gains for the whole building require such provision and the HVAC plant sized accordingly.

This is the dilemma facing the designers of both new buildings and refurbishment projects. The correct assumptions must be made for loading densities and the designs should not be restricted simply to incorporating more and more energy-using HVAC equipment.

5.9 Environmental moderating systems

Reference to Section 7.7 will provide a more complete explanation of the different thermal moderating systems that can be incorporated into buildings. In addition, lighting systems need to be considered when examining the whole impact of energy use in an internal space. According to the Building Research Establishment 'In offices, for example, the lighting often accounts for around 50 per cent of the electricity used, and lighting costs can exceed those for heating' [12]. Careful consideration of the performance of lighting equipment and controls can reduce energy consumption significantly while maintaining appropriate lighting levels.

Techniques such as 'thermal storage' or 'night-time purging' (see Section 7.7) can improve the overall efficiency of HVAC systems while the introduction of building management systems and lighting level control can save energy by better utilisation. However, the realisation is gradually dawning that energy use should not be viewed in isolation and that a global environmental matrix exists such that each element is interdependent on the others in order for efficiency to be maximised.

Energy remains comparatively cheap but the consequences of CFC use and ozone layer depletion or greenhouse gases on global warming outweigh any cost consideration, let alone future exhaustion of fossil fuel resources. Therefore, the impetus to save environmentally unfriendly energy sources will come from directions other than purely greater cost or depletion, for example a growing desire to mitigate environmental impact.

The requirement to introduce artificial tempering within buildings is dealt with later in this chapter. Assuming that some form of conditioning is necessary, it is useful to look briefly at the main systems available before considering the energy implications of the most common HVAC systems.

Variable air volume (VAV) systems

Single-duct VAV systems are generally considered to be the most economical variant where large open-plan spaces exist. However, the creation of a cellular office layout can give rise to the need for costly modification if satisfactory environmental conditions are to be maintained. VAV boxes are normally installed within the ceiling void, those at the perimeter being fitted with heating coils to allow for perimeter heating. Chilled air is ducted to the VAV boxes and then reheated in the perimeter zones as required, to maintain room conditions. The central plant comprises boilers and refrigeration equipment together with primary air-handling units. The air-handling units respond to the VAV boxes indirectly through the ductwork system by maintaining a static discharge pressure in the system. This allows the system to reduce fan volume thus saving operational electrical power costs.

Fan coil unit (FCU) systems

An FCU system can be installed either in suspended ceiling voids or under window sills around the perimeter of a building. Heating is normally provided from centrally located modular boilers and cooling from similarly positioned refrigeration plant. Separate air-handling units introduce fresh air into the FCUs with exhaust air being taken out of the building via ceiling-mounted diffusers.

Unitary heat pump (UHP) system

A UHP system is one of many decentralised systems that are alternatives to FCU systems. The majority of decentralised systems rely solely upon on-peak electricity as the primary fuel which results in much higher energy costs in use than a centralised system (such as VAV) which uses the efficiency of large plant and more economical fuel sources like gas, oil and off-peak electricity for heating. Where UHP systems have an advantage is that they rely upon equipment with high coefficient of performance (COP) characteristics enabling the best use to be made of the (expensive) on-peak electricity.

Direct expansion (DX) heat pump system

A DX heat pump system is one of many decentralised systems that are alternatives to FCU systems. The majority of decentralised systems rely solely upon on-peak electricity as the primary fuel which results in much higher energy costs in use than a centralised system (such as VAV) which uses the efficiency of large plant and more economical fuel sources like gas, oil and off-peak electricity for heating. DX systems do not have the advantage of high COP characteristics which enable the best use to be made of on-peak electricity and therefore are comparatively expensive to run. Designed originally for single-unit applications, DX systems are not appropriate for large areas.

Variable refrigerant volume (VRV) multi-system heat pump

A VRV heat pump system is similar in many ways to the UHP system. The systems rely upon on-peak electricity and the equipment has high COP characteristics to enable the best use to be made of on-peak electricity. The VRV system provides heating and cooling via the use of refrigerant, similar to the DX heat pump system, utilising indoor and outdoor units. The VRV system, however, is a modular system which permits the installation of one condenser unit to serve several indoor units via a common refrigerant pipework system. The outdoor unit contains the refrigeration compressor, condenser fans and associated controls; it can be considered a partially centralised system. The in-door unit, containing the air-handling fan, filter and controls, can either be a cassette-type unit, installed through the ceiling, or a fan coil-type unit, installed within the ceiling void.

There are many publications which adequately deal with the energy requirements and comparisons of the various HVAC systems described in this section. The most authoritative source of information is the Building Services Research and Information Association [13] which regularly produces journals and publications.

The difficulty in giving energy guidance regarding HVAC systems stems from the variation in building types in which the various systems are installed. In general terms, however, Table 5.2 gives normalised cost ratios.

Relative capital and running costs of the different HVAC systems are undeniably important but the wider issue is to question the validity of current design assumptions; the approach must be to design buildings that reduce the need for mechanical systems. So how should the responsible environmental engineer advise a client or fellow-professional?

5.10 A holistic approach

The criteria that should be uppermost in the project team's mind must relate to the whole building, not just individual elements: a philosophy also raised in Chapter 4, on architecture and landscape. This holistic approach to design necessitates a review of current design practices and priorities.

The real problem should be not 'what to do with the waste energy' but 'how can we stop the proliferation of excess energy usage'. Build-ings are being designed to accommodate major equipment loads. Offices especially suffer from the 'maximum density equals total de-mand' maxim. This is notoriously wrong. The increasing usage of

Table 5.2   *Normalised cost ratios for HVAC systems.*

HVAC system	Relative cost ratio	
	Capital	*Electrical running*
VAV plus perimeter heating	1.0	1.0
4-pipe fan coil and ducted air system	0.97	2.18
UHP system plus ducted fresh air	0.95	1.33
DX heat pump system without ducted air	0.9	1.4
VRV multi-system heat pump without fresh air	0.96	1.25

computers, IT and workstation peripherals means that loads of 100 Wm^2 are quite commonplace. HVAC systems are being installed to compensate for such loads. If such densities are not being achieved then the large HVAC plant runs acutely inefficiently and draws large electrical loading. If such densities are proved in use then the proliferation must be curtailed by using more efficient equipment.

In general, with some excellent exceptions, the technology associated with energy efficiency in office buildings has been developed as an 'add-on' to the high-energy-using systems. This is the result of the historic approach to building design. In the vast majority of cases, the external aesthetic design of the building is the overriding planning approval issue. Thus the environmental systems are designed to counteract the effects of the architecture, rather than to complement or interact with the building concept. Computerised management systems operating in conjunction with intelligent controllers enable systems to respond to building requirements. Lighting levels can be modulated, temperatures controlled, motor speeds varied and complete.systems monitored constantly. Technology has developed such that, if budgets permit, we can control and monitor every energy-using piece of equipment that can be fitted into a building.

Computerised management systems are undeniably useful in minimising the environmental impact of buildings by ensuring that systems operate efficiently. However, they are typically used as an 'add-on' to high-energy-using systems rather than as part of a holistic approach.

There are many studies which show that modern office building energy costs are completely dominated by the activities going on inside, rather than the design of the building shell. Significantly, computer installations and their associated air conditioning can be the largest and most expensive energy user. There are also cases where the energy bill for lighting exceeds the energy bill for heating. Efforts to reduce window area to minimise heat loss and gain can result in the increased use of artificial lighting which can use up to three times the energy of the heating.

In a similar way, the reduction in overall thermal transmittance (U value) in the Building Regulations 1991 for thermal insulation in the UK may not suit all situations. A large proportion of modern buildings have high heat loads due to office equipment, lighting, etc. Air conditioning is frequently used to reduce the temperature to acceptable levels. If the building retains more heat due to better insulation, then the air-conditioning system has to work harder to remove the heat gain, greatly increasing the overall energy use of the building. Nevertheless, failure to provide an adequate level of thermal insulation to building envelopes can result in unacceptable environmental conditions in the space adjacent to external walls. Thus, the best solution is to attempt to minimise heat gains from equipment, etc, rather than responding in an inappropriate way.

It is important to emphasise that continued improvements in the efficiency of environmental systems are very necessary, but these improvements in efficiency will be lost unless we change our approach to building design and the way in which the internal environment can be controlled by suitable structural elements.

5.11 Buildings in equilibrium

It is becoming more evident that internal heat gains within office buildings are going to be much lower than predicted and it is likely that future generations of office equipment will produce even less heat. The potential for servicing buildings without full air conditioning in the temperate UK will therefore increase. Air conditioning typically doubles building energy usage, and the scope for savings is enormous in running as well as capital costs.

We are moving into a new era of energy awareness and building design expectations. The individual needs and requirements of building users will be important factors and will become the driving force. This new era will require use of recent technological advances in building shell design, services equipment, control systems and computer-aided facilities management. The combination of computer technology and advanced materials will ensure energy efficiency combined with the required standards of control and comfort.

Further developments are being made in the way window glass performs as a transmitter of solar and visible radiation into buildings. Also, improvements in glazing U valves are being achieved, reducing heat loss from buildings. Chapter 4, on architecture and landscape, explores these issues. There are indications too that glass will also play a key role in IT, utilising glass for information display, reducing the energy heat emissions of the present systems. The reductions possible in the heat emissions from buildings combined with the intelligent building skin responding to the internal environment will permit a return to the natural equilibrium. It will be possible to have complete interaction of the inside and outside lighting and temperature systems, truly reducing the energy costs. Efficiency improvements with the use of night-time cooling or thermal storage systems will further improve the overall building efficiency.

External shading devices have a great influence in reducing cooling and lighting energy consumption. Integrating these devices into computer management systems is already possible. However, an improvement in the operation, reliability and appearance will be required if their continued use in the future is to occur. Yet, if landscaping design is integrated with building design it is possible to shade buildings in summer by foliage from vines or trees, with the deciduous varieties allowing light and heat through during the winter months. It is also possible to utilise high-transpiring varieties of trees, such as the aspen tree, to create evaporative cooling, or to use shrubs and plants to remove pollutants from the air that we breathe. This approach has been termed 'buildings in equilibrium' because it adds the missing dimension to the creation of dwelling places for human need by balancing naturally occurring phenomena with contemporary materials and concepts.

It may well be that the ecological safety of our planet, personal comfort and human health issues are the impetus we require to save energy. Buildings are one of the highest users of energy on a global basis. We must revise our attitude to their creation if we are to avoid perpetuating the errors of the past.

By examining the materials and systems we use and by defining the user requirements first – developing from the inside–out – we can incorporate the concept of 'buildings in equilibrium' to achieve micro- and macro-economic compatibility.

5.12 Life cycle costing

A traditional criticism of British property-making decisions is that they are taken on the basis of initial, or capital, cost and do not take running costs into account. This approach militates against energy conservation as developers and investors of commercial buildings for speculative letting do not tend to have a direct interest in energy bills, as these are met by occupants on full repairing and insuring terms. However, this attitude is beginning to change, especially in a depressed property market where tenants' demands for buildings with low running costs must be taken seriously. A way of doing this is to adopt life cycle costing, which applies to existing or proposed buildings, or parts of buildings.

Life cycle costing is the present value of costs incurred over the life of a building (or at least the life of one party's interest in it). These costs include the construction costs, running costs and the value or costs arising from disposal. It is important to note that all costs are discounted to present value, because costs and receipts at some point in the future are less valuable than if received now. Further mention of this subject is given in Chapter 4, on architecture and landscape.

Life cycle costing is useful as it allows all costs to be identified and this can be used as a management tool for decision making. In particular, it enables effective choice between different options. An example, so far as energy efficiency is concerned, is the choice between the present value of meeting building regulation standards of thermal insulation or selecting an enhanced specification with the benefit of lower fuel bills; life cycle costing is a procedure for reviewing trade-offs between initial and running costs such as this. It will be readily appreciated that different criteria will have to be adopted for different circumstances. For instance, an owner occupier who plans to retain interest in a building for the foreseeable future will select a different time period for the life cycle costing exercise than an occupier who proposes to enter into, say, a 15-year lease. The following procedure may be useful in implementing life cycle costing:

1. Establish the objectives, for example, to reduce fuel bills by a particular amount.
2. Choose the method for achieving the objective (consider all realistic possibilities).
3. Gather the data required.
4. Formulate assumptions such as forecast escalation of energy costs.
5. Identify the costs and the life cycle.
6. Consider costs and rank the alternatives, using an appropriate technique.
7. Carry out a sensitivity analysis when the results of the previous steps do not produce an alternative which is clearly preferable.
8. Investigate capital cost constraints.

Life cycle costing has four components, two of which apply to proposed buildings or components, with the remainder applying to existing buildings or components. Looking first at proposed work, life cycle

The sequence linking LCCA, LCCP and LCCM

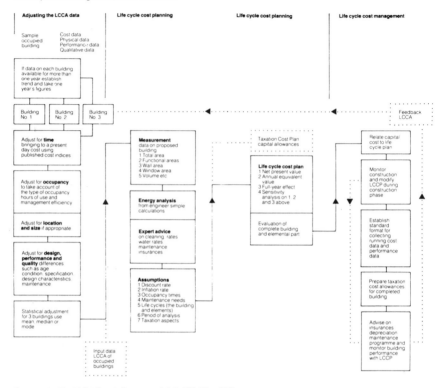

Diagram reproduced from "Life Cycle Costing for Construction" published by RICS 1983 pp. 74-75

Figure 5.2   Relationship between the different components of life cycle costings. (Reproduced from Life Cycle Costing for Construction *published by RICS, 1983, pp. 74–5.)*

cost planning (LCCP) is used to establish estimated targets for running costs, to allow particular methods of achieving the objective to be selected. Full-year effect costs also apply to proposed work, but are used to identify short-term running costs. Now, turning to existing buildings and their components, life cycle cost analysis (LCCA) identifies their running costs. Life cycle cost management (LCCM) is based on life cycle cost analysis and is a tool for identifying where there is scope for reducing running costs. Figure 5.2 shows the relationship between the different components of life cycle costings.

It can be seen that life cycle costing is useful for a range of applications. Obviously, it is essential that the correct technique is applied in each case. The techniques are not a replacement for decision making, as the results will vary considerably depending upon the data which is used and the assumptions that are made. Furthermore, there are some difficulties in implementing life cycle cost techniques. It is not appropriate to consider these here, but reference should be made to a text on life cycle costing before using it.

5.13 Summary

- Energy consumed through our use of buildings is a significant contributor to environmental costs such as global warming and acid rain. There is increasing pressure to enhance energy efficiency to reduce pollution.
- Many energy efficiency measures are cost effective.
- There is an argument that inefficient buildings will become less desirable and therefore less valuable.
- Regulations and legislation affecting energy performance are becoming more stringent and it does not take a great stretch of the imagination to anticipate that more efficient energy use may become mandatory.
- There are many components to the energy efficiency of buildings, from the insulation standard of building fabric to the performance of services plant. All of these aspects must be considered during design and construction, occupation and maintenance.
- The starting point for determining the level of insulation for new buildings is the building regulations. The Approved Document suggests a number of ways for meeting the required level of performance.
- Levels of thermal insulation required of new buildings have increased and this process is likely to continue, especially with forthcoming legislation from the European Commission.
- There is a strong argument for using greater levels of thermal insulation in new buildings than the Building Regulations 1991 demand. However, the level adopted will depend upon a number of factors and each building should be considered separately.
- High levels of thermal insulation may result in non-traditional construction and materials. Care should be taken to minimise the risk of failure.
- Materials from local sources should be chosen wherever possible in order to minimise the energy consumed during the journey to site.
- The processing and manufacture of building materials uses energy. Little information is available, but in general terms the greater the amount of processing the more energy is used. This should be borne in mind when choices are made.
- At the design stage, care should be taken to maximise durability

and flexibility in order to avoid premature failure or obsolescence.

- Out-of-town schemes usually imply a high degree of fuel use in transporting building users from their homes; therefore, the whole scheme may be very inefficient in energy terms.
- The way in which we have viewed the investment potential of buildings has maintained the proliferation of energy-dependent internal environments and stifled the introduction of more natural methods of moderating occupied spaces.
- HVAC and other artificial environmental moderators are very high energy users. The 'bolt on' energy-saving measures that are available may well be contributing to the overall reduction in energy usage, but to make real strides, radical approaches are required. The eradication of artificial environmental conditioning using the building itself as the environmental moderator is the way forward.
- A holistic approach to building creation can easily make inroads into the very heart of energy use and can provide the platform for encouraging buildings in equilibrium.
- There is a trade-off between initial and running costs, or the costs of energy-saving measures against fuel bills. Life cycle costing is a procedure for identifying the present value of total costs throughout the life of the building which allows effective decision making between different options.

References

1. S. Curwell, C. March and R. Venables (eds), *Buildings and Health – The Rosehaugh Guide to the Design, Construction, Use and Management of Buildings* (London: RIBA Publications, 1990) p. 450; and 'Feature – RIBA conference discusses greenhouse effect', *Energy Management* (April/May 1990) p. 18.
2. G. Henderson and L. D. Shorrock, *BRE Information Paper 2/90 Greenhouse–gas Emissions and Buildings in the United Kingdom* (Watford: BRE, 1990).
3. Secretaries of State for Environment, Trade and Industry, Health, Education and Science, Scotland, Transport, Energy and Northern Ireland, the Minister for Agriculture, Fisheries and Food and the Secretaries of State for Employment and Wales, *This Common Inheritance – Britain's Environmental Strategy* (London: HMSO, September 1990) p. 71.
4. C. Cookson, 'Battle for fuel efficiency', *Financial Times – Survey Industry and the Environment* (16 March 1990) p. iii.
5. D. Hargreaves, 'In the fires of adversity', *Financial Times – Survey Energy Efficiency* (16 October 1991) p. i.
6. 'Good Practice Case Study 15 – Energy Efficiency in Offices', *Best*

Practice Programme by Energy Efficiency Office, Department of Energy (July 1990) p. 4.

7. Department of the Environment and the Welsh Office, *The Building Regulations 1991, Conservation of Fuel and Power, Approved Document L1* (London: HMSO, 1991).
8. Eurima European Insulation Manufacturers' Association, *Thermal Insulation Standards in Housing in Europe* (Brussels: Eurima, July 1991).
9. Eurisol UK Mineral Wool Association, *Reducing the Greenhouse Effect by Domestic Insulation* (St Albans: Eurisol, 1991) p. 5.
10. G. Jones for National Economic Development Office, *Building with British Products – How to Sell More British Building, DIY and Hardware Products* (London: NEDO, September 1988) pp. 7–9.
11. S. Curwell, C. March and R. Venables (eds), *Buildings and Health – The Rosehaugh Guide to the Design, Construction, Use and Management of Buildings* (London: RIBA Publications, 1990) p. 447.
12. Building Research Energy Conservation Support Unit, *Best Practice Programme. General Information Leaflet 6. Energy Efficiency in Lighting* (Watford: BRE, 1992).
13. Building Services Research and Information Association, Old Bracknell Lane West, Bracknell, Berkshire RG12 4AH, tel: 0344 426511.

Further reading

Building Research Establishment, *Thermal Insulation: Avoiding the Risks – A guide to Good Practice Building Construction* (Watford: BRE and HMSO, 1989).

CIBSE Guide – Volumes A, B, C (London: Chartered Institution of Building Services Engineers, 1988 and updates).

S. Curwell, C. March and R. Venables (eds), *Buildings and Health – The Rosehaugh Guide to the Design, Construction, Use and Management of Buildings* (London: RIBA Publications, 1990).

Department of the Environment and the Welsh Office, *The Building Regulations 1991, Conservation of Fuel and Power, Approved Document L1* (London: HMSO, 1991).

N. Dudley, *Good Health on a Polluted Planet* (London: Thorsons, 1991).

'Energy and the environment survey', *The Economist* (31 August 1991) pp. 5–44.

Eurisol UK Mineral Wool Association, *Reducing the Greenhouse Effect by Domestic Insulation* (St Albans: Eurisol, 1991).

R. Flanagan and G. Norman, *Life Cycle Costing for Construction* (London: Surveyors' Publications, July 1983).

R. Flanagan, G. Norman, J. Meadows and G. Robinson, *Life Cycle*

Costing – Theory and Practice (Oxford: BSP Professional Books, 1989).

G. J. Hughes (ed.), *Electricity and Buildings* (London: Peter Peregrinus Ltd, 1984).

Hunkin, *Almost Everything There is to Know* (London: Octopus Ltd, 1990).

D. Pearson, *The Natural House Book* (London: Conran Octopus Ltd, 1989).

S. Rock (ed.), *Director's Guide to Energy Management* (London: The Director Publications Ltd, September 1991).

6 Building Materials
Stuart Johnson

6.1 Introduction

Many of us are now in the habit of ferrying our empty bottles and yesterday's newspapers to the recycling bins in our lead-free fuelled cars. This concern for the environment is beginning to change the way we behave during working hours, too. For all sorts of reasons, lots of companies are beginning to formulate environmental policies which influence the way in which they use their buildings. Reasons for adopting these policies vary, ranging from a desire on the part of occupiers of space to create a healthy environment for their workforce and customers, to a perception by developers that they must create buildings with a minimal environmental impact to meet the demands of an increasingly discerning market.

So, increased environmental concern is being translated into action particularly by the formulation of environmental policies. Such policies usually stipulate that building materials are to be specified in an environmentally aware manner, both for the maintenance of existing property and the construction of new schemes. Unfortunately, there are difficulties in actually implementing such a policy and these are explored in this chapter.

Building materials affect the environment in different ways. Some affect the external, or global, environment, such as chlorofluorocarbons and tropical hardwood from non-sustainable sources, whereas others affect the environment within the buildings, including the use of asbestos products and solvent-based paints. This chapter examines the use of tropical hardwoods, chlorofluorocarbons, asbestos, paints, timber treatments, formaldehyde and recycled materials. There are, of course, environmental aspects to the use of other materials which should be considered before they are specified, perhaps using the principles identified here.

The environment does not lend itself to simple right-or-wrong selection criteria of materials; therefore, this chapter should not be used to compile a schedule of proscribed materials. There is a temptation to add environmental issues to the list of deleterious materials prohibited under many development agreements and other documents – this should be avoided. An example of the flexible approach required can be given in the case of asbestos. Sometimes, asbestos is difficult to substitute as alternatives are generally more expensive and may lack some of its inherent qualities. Asbestos is still used in new work very occasionally, for example where the amounts are small and unlikely to be released into the air such as with putties or plastics; therefore, its use should not be dismissed entirely so long as caution is adopted.

6.2 Tropical hardwoods

Tropical rain forests are being lost at an unacceptable rate for a variety of reasons, including our desire to use tropical hardwoods in construction. However, deforestation is not due solely to timber exports. It also occurs when hardwoods are used locally as fuel and for construction, and sites are cleared to allow for crops and grazing as well as mining. Scientists believe that the most significant effect of the destruction of the tropical rain forests is the influence on global climatic patterns. Much clearing of the rain forests is by burning, which releases large amounts of the greenhouse gas carbon dioxide and thereby contributes to global warming. Forests act as a 'green lung' because as trees grow they absorb carbon dioxide and emit oxygen. Therefore, burning of the forests not only results in the emission of carbon dioxide but also removes a source of oxygen.

Another criticism of deforestation is that it often leads to soil erosion which renders the land useless for sustainable agriculture. Also, loss of forest destroys natural habitats with the risk that some species of plants and animals will become extinct, with the consequent loss of potential developments in medicine and other fields. Lastly, deforestation results in only short-term economic gain for the exporting countries as it generally involves a once-and-for-all gain with the destruction of the forest. Thus, whilst the export of tropical hardwoods for use in the construction industry is not the only cause of deforestation, it is a contributor and care must be taken when timber is selected to minimise destruction.

It is especially important to avoid specifying endangered species. Information on which timbers to avoid can be found in *The Good Wood Guide* by Friends of the Earth and *The Real Wood Guide* by Timber Trades Federation. Many would argue that merely avoiding endangered species of timber does not go far enough and that all tropical hardwood specified should be from sustainably managed plantations, that is, for felling to be carried out in such a way that long-term production is not prejudiced. The guides mentioned will help to identify the species which may be obtained from sustainable sources and, having selected a type of timber, the following model specification clause could be adopted:

Model specification clause

All references to tropical hardwoods contained within the specification are to be obtained exclusively from sustainable sources. The contractor is to provide evidence, by a supplier's certificate and labelling for each consignment delivered to site, that the timber is from such a source.

The certificate and the label should include the following information:

(a) The source of the timber.
(b) Evidence that the source is sustainable.
(c) Timber species.

The Good Wood Seal of Approval by Friends of the Earth would suffice. Information on appropriate suppliers can be obtained from the Timber Trades Federation, Friends of the Earth and International Timber Trades Organisation.

There is increasing demand for timber from sustainable sources and this is likely to lead to an increased availability. For example, the International Timber Trades Organisation has a campaign, called Project 2000, with the aim that all tropical hardwood exports are from sustainable sources by the year 2000. Nevertheless, at present, demand for tropical hardwoods from sustainable sources outstrips supply. If difficulties are encountered in obtaining supplies of tropical hardwoods from a sustainable source, one course of action is to restrict the use of tropical hardwoods to limited areas of buildings, such as an entrance hall or boardroom, whilst using alternative materials elsewhere. This is not an ideal state of affairs, but does at least reduce the use of tropical hardwoods from non-sustainable sources to a minimum. A feature of the trend to enhance the standard of finishes, particularly for commercial buildings, has been the increasingly extensive use of hardwood joinery where previously painted softwood would have been used.

Alternatives to tropical hardwoods include timber from temperate climates which tend to be sustainably produced, although this is not always the case. It makes environmental (and economic) sense to ensure that all timber is produced sustainably, including hardwoods and softwoods from temperate climates. Thus, when specifying any timber, care should be taken to ascertain its source. This can be done by using a modified form of the model specification clause referred to earlier. Timber merchants can provide the documentary evidence required. Metal, plastic and processed wood products, or less traditional detailing removing the need for timber, such as carpet skirtings, can also be adopted. Care should be taken with the selection of alternatives as these may have other environmental implications, such as the consumption of large amounts of energy during production. Tropical hardwoods are imported in a variety of forms, including as processed boards such as plywood. When using these boards, care should be taken to ensure that they do not incorporate tropical hardwoods from a non-sustainable source.

Where tropical hardwood joinery has been used in existing buildings, it is pointless to consider replacement as the damage to the environment has already taken place. Indeed, it can be argued that to strip out existing tropical hardwood joinery is environmentally damaging as it will involve disposal of existing materials (possibly resulting in the release of carbon dioxide). Also, procuring alternatives will create pollution by processing and transporting the replacement material.

6.3 Chlorofluorocarbons

It is now acknowledged that the man-made chemicals, chlorofluorocarbons (CFCs), contribute to depletion of the ozone layer and also add to the greenhouse effect. These phenomena are explored in Chapter 2, on environmental issues. In the construction industry, CFCs and associated compounds are used in insulation materials, fire-extinguishing systems, air-conditioning plant and refrigeration equipment. They are also found in some packaging foams, aerosol sprays and soft furnishings.

CFC-blown insulants take the form of rigid urethane, extruded polystyrene and phenolic foams. They may be found in insulated exterior doors, sprayed insulation for underground pipes, and thermal insulation materials used in building fabric and service installations. CFC-blown insulants currently have about 10 per cent by weight of the British insulation market [1]. Other insulation materials include mineral fibre (which has the largest market share) and expanded polystyrene.

CFC-blown insulants should be avoided wherever possible – this usually entails simple substitution with an alternative material. However, this is not always straightforward as some applications rely upon CFC-blown insulants' inherent water resistance, such as with insulation below ground level, inverted roofs or to line the external faces of walls. In such cases, it is possible to substitute other types of thermal insulation although these are not always tried and tested, with the risk that they may fail. Alternatively, a different design solution can be adopted which removes the need for thermal insulation with waterproof qualities. Manufacturers are developing and beginning to launch insulants blown with other gases including carbon dioxide and hydrochlorofluorocarbons (HCFCs) but these have some short-comings. In particular, they may be less efficient at providing thermal insulation and, of course, HCFCs contribute towards ozone depletion and global warming, albeit to a much lesser extent than CFCs. Therefore, before specifying one of the new generation of blown insulants, care must be taken to consider its performance, both initially and over time.

With CFC-blown insulants, the emission of CFCs occurs during manufacture and upon destruction, with slow emission during the lifetime of the foam. Where CFC-blown insulants have been used in existing buildings, it is not usually appropriate to remove them because they are often in an inaccessible location. However, when such insulants are exposed, such as upon reroofing, the opportunity could be taken to provide an alternative type of insulation and to destroy the CFC-blown foam in a controlled way. In practice, the desirability of this course of action is debatable as it may prove difficult to arrange suitable disposal. Furthermore, the resources consumed by the replacement insulation must be considered. CFCs are used in other building components, particularly some fire-extinguishing systems and air-conditioning plant.

6.4 Asbestos

Asbestos is a naturally occurring fibrous material which is effective as a fire-resisting, thermal and electrical-insulating material. It has also been used as a filler in a wide range of products, including some paints, flexible floor coverings, cladding panels, gutters and flue pipes. It has been, and continues to be, a great contributor to human safety. However, exposure to the microscopic fibres can constitute a serious health risk – it is associated with several terminal diseases, including asbestosis and lung cancer.

The health risk arises by the inhalation of the microscopic fibres. The air-borne fibre concentration is dependent upon the type, form, friability, condition and location; thus, not all asbestos constitutes an immediate risk. The risk of contracting disease is low, but any level of exposure is usually considered unacceptable. Where a health risk is established, there are two courses of action. Firstly, removal of the asbestos and replacement with a substitute material. Secondly, encapsulation or sealing of the asbestos fibres. The course of action adopted will depend upon whether the asbestos is in sound condition and undisturbed and whether it is likely to remain that way. It must also be recognised that the presence of asbestos is an emotive subject and the owner of the building or its occupiers may decide on a course of action for other than technical reasons.

Figure 6.1 provides an outline of the procedure to be adopted following the discovery of asbestos. It is essential that such work is only carried out by licensed specialist firms, under strictly controlled conditions with fibre levels regularly monitored. A number of regulations apply including the Control of Asbestos at Work Regulations 1987 which sets out precautions to be applied to work with any exposure to any form of asbestos. If asbestos fibres beyond given limits are likely to be released, additional regulations apply. Familiarity with regulations applying to work with asbestos and disposal of asbestos waste is essential before any work is carried out.

There is some concern that alternatives to asbestos may also present health problems. Current research indicates that health effects of mineral fibres are restricted to irritation of the eyes, skin and throat which can be overcome by protection. Whilst there is currently no evidence of a link between lung cancer and mineral fibres, it is likely that research will continue, but in the meantime recommendations for protection of operatives should be followed closely [2].

6.5 Paints

Solvent-based paints

Many paints, including most glosses and eggshells, are based upon solvents such as white spirit. It is alleged that these can result in respiratory and neurological disorders to painters and building occupiers. Whilst there are controls in some countries, in the UK studies of the risk are at an early stage and the use of solvent-based paints is not prohibited, although regulations apply such as the Control of Substances Hazardous to Health (COSHH) [3].

There is special cause for concern where solvent-based paints are used inside buildings where, even with mechanical ventilation especially installed for the duration of the works, the level of solvents in the air may be excessive. COSHH requires a clear understanding of the

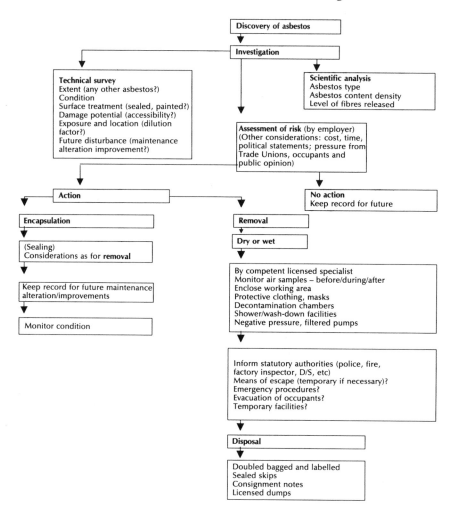

Figure 6.1 Outline of the procedure to be followed on discovery of asbestos. (Reproduced from Watts' Pocket Handbook 1991, *Watts & Partners, 1990, pp. 112–13.)*

effects of solvent-based paints on painters and reduction of the risk by the use of, say, protective clothing and mechanical ventilation equipment. An alternative is to use a material which is not solvent based.

Availability of water-based products is improving rapidly with manufacturers responding to demands for healthier materials and changes in regulations. As an example, Dulux offers a range of water-based products including eggshell, gloss and floor paints. Of course, other products have traditionally been water based such as emulsion paints.

Whilst these new materials are undoubtedly useful, particularly within buildings where traditional materials can lead to unacceptable solvent levels in the air, they are not universally appropriate. At present, water-based paints have some drawbacks and the manufacturers continue to recommend the use of solvent-based paints in certain circumstances: firstly, for external surfaces because solvent-based gloss is more durable and, secondly, for radiators and other heated metal surfaces where water-based gloss may soften. As stated earlier, where solvent-based paints are used protective measures may be necessary.

Over time the availability and performance of water-based paints will improve and the range of suitable uses will increase. Indeed, Dulux aims that, by the year 2000, all of their products will be water based, with solvent-based paints no longer being available. Therefore, when arranging decoration, it is important to become aware of the range of products available and the uses that are likely to be successful.

Where solvent-based paints have been used in buildings, there is little cause for alarm as the excessive levels of solvent in the air occur during and immediately after painting. Nevertheless, when redecoration is needed the use of water-based products should be considered and specified in the same manner as for new work.

Lead-based paints

Historically, lead-based paints were used for their purity of colour and durability. The adverse effects on human health with the use of lead-based paints are by no means a recent discovery; regulations controlling the use of such paints date from the 1920s in Britain. Today, poisoning is rare and, typically, only occurs during careless removal when high levels of dust containing lead can be generated and also when children chew on joinery which has been decorated with this type of paint.

Lead is no longer used in paint for do-it-yourself sale, although it is found in a limited range of specialist products. Paints containing lead have two principal uses: as primers for metalwork and for work to historic buildings. In the latter form, lead-based paints are favoured because of their purity of colour, durability and other unique characteristics. Bodies such as the English Heritage and the Society for the Protection of Ancient Buildings are anxious that this specialist use should be allowed to continue. In summary, lead-based paints are very rarely used for new work, but where there is a strong argument that their unique characteristics outweigh the possible risk to health they should only be used with extreme caution. In particular, the Lead at Work Regulations 1980 and COSHH regulations should be adhered to.

Although old lead-based paints may exhibit a cubed surface pattern, the only reliable way of identifying the presence of lead is by laboratory analysis. It should be appreciated that even where lead is detected, the best course of action is not necessarily its removal. The risk to human health from lead is minimal if the paint surface is sound. In such cases, unless the areas are accessible to children, redecoration with a lead-free paint system would be acceptable. Where paint containing lead must be removed, either because of the presence of children or because the paint surface is unsound, care must be taken with the method adopted. The aim must be to minimise the release of lead. Wet sanding and chemical paint strippers are the preferred methods and, even then, protective clothing and adequate ventilation are needed.

6.6 Timber treatments

Pesticides are used as timber treatments to guard against insect attack and rot. Timber treatments are useful in prolonging the life of many timber building elements, but unfortunately there are health risks associated with most treatments, both to those applying them and to building occupants. There are also potentially detrimental effects to plants, animals and the environment. Many materials can be toxic, including lindane and PCP (pentachlorophenol). From 1 July 1992, government approval for the use of PCP has been withdrawn (with some exceptions).

Obviously, where such materials are to be used the applicator should be protected, work areas sealed and, where possible, the use should be avoided in areas which are occupied. The Health and Safety Commission produces a useful document entitled 'The safe use of pesticides for non-agricultural purposes' which is an approved code of practice under the Health and Safety at Work, etc, Act 1974 as well as being one of the ways of satisfying COSHH regulations [4]. Practical guidance is given on the use of pesticides in buildings, whether application is *in situ* or by pre-treatment. TRADA has an information sheet which explores why timber preservation is necessary and goes on to explore the main chemicals and processes used [5]. This document provides useful background information to allow an informed decision to be taken.

It would be wise to avoid the use of materials which can be toxic, but unfortunately there are few tried and tested alternatives, although less harmful pesticides will become available gradually. Therefore, the practical approach is to use the pesticides in a controlled manner, both by reference to the relevant regulations and also by careful identification of timbers requiring treatment in preference to treating all areas. Another approach is to eliminate the need for timber treatments by careful design and detailing of timbers, with particular attention to damp-proofing and protection. An example of this approach, so far as timber window frames are concerned, is that treatment can be avoided by the prudent selection of window sections which ensure that rainwater is shed quickly, in conjunction with a thorough redecoration regime. The success of this approach can be maximised by setting window frames back from the face of the surrounding walls and thereby reducing the degree of exposure of the timber.

6.7 Formaldehyde

Urea formaldehyde foam cavity insulation

Urea formaldehyde foam is a common form of cavity wall insulation. Unfortunately, formaldehyde vapour arising from this insulation can give rise to a number of symptoms in the building occupants. In particular, irritation to the throat, nose and eyes after injection of the foam which can, in extreme cases, continue for a number of years. It is also a suspected cause of cancer.

Building regulations require that urea formaldehyde foam cavity insulation shall not give off sufficient formaldehyde vapour within the building to cause symptoms of irritation [6]. In simple terms, this means the inner leaf of a cavity wall should be built of blockwork or brickwork and be imperforate. There are additional requirements on the type of material and the way it is installed. Thus, urea formaldehyde foam insulation should not be applied with timber-framed construction where the cavity is required to ventilate the frame, or with other forms of construction where the inner leaf is not of blockwork or some other masonry.

With existing buildings, where this type of cavity insulation has been installed and occupants complain of the symptoms of exposure to excessive levels of formaldehyde vapour, the initial task is to provide increased ventilation. This is especially important with modern buildings where efficient draught stripping tends to reduce the number of air changes. The opportunity should then be taken to verify the integrity of the inner leaf of the cavity. Openings should be sealed, often after the removal of surplus foam which has collected in voids such as roof spaces and behind baths. To avoid skin irritation, protective clothing should be worn when removing surplus foam.

One of the reasons for adopting a cavity wall construction is that there is a lower risk of damp penetration than with solid walls. For this reason, it seems strange to construct walls with a cavity and then fill it.

This concern is substantiated by a guide produced by the National Federation of Building Trades Employers which states that there have been a significant number of complaints about damp penetration through cavity walls insulated with urea formaldehyde foam [7]. This sets out the conditions for successful use of the foam, including height, detailing and degree of exposure of the walls. To summarise, with new construction it would seem that there are preferable ways of enhancing the thermal insulation, such as partial cavity fill or lining the inside face of the inner leaf. Similarly, with existing buildings there are other methods of increasing the thermal efficiency of walls, such as lining the outside or inside faces of the walls, or, where it is desirable to insulate the cavity, other methods are available.

Other uses of formaldehyde

Formaldehyde is used as an adhesive in processed timber boards like plywood, medium-density fibreboard and chipboard. As with foam for cavity insulation, there is concern about the health aspects of exposure to formaldehyde vapour which depends not only on the performance of the boards, but also their extent and the way in which the building is ventilated and occupied. Whilst maximum exposure rates are now generally accepted, there are no controls in Britain (except in factories where formaldehyde is used). Especial concern is reserved for chipboard and medium-density fibreboard because emission continues for a long time. Where there is a desire to avoid high formaldehyde levels in buildings there are two options: either specification of low-emission boards or treatment of boards. Low-emission particle boards are known as E1 type (to the German standard). An alternative is to seal boards, for example with melamine or varnish – it is important to treat both faces and the edges. The Timber Research and Development Association produces a useful advisory sheet [8]. It is worth noting that formaldehyde is also found in other products, including some carpets.

6.8 Recycled materials

There are finite supplies of almost all building materials and consequently there are sound environmental reasons for using second-hand and recycled building components wherever possible. Not only will the use of these materials extend the time for which finite supplies will be available, but it will also conserve energy and other resources which would otherwise be consumed in the production of new materials; every ton of glass recycled saves 30 gallons (or about 136 litres) of oil [9]. Obviously, second-hand or recycled products are not always available, but to minimise the environmental impact and cost of building operations there is an obligation to keep abreast of new developments. As with the selection of any other product, there is no reason why recycled and second-hand materials cannot meet specific performance criteria; there is no benefit in using a recycled or second-hand product if it will fail prematurely and give rise to the need for costly remedial work.

The use of recycled or second-hand materials is only one way of getting maximum use from building products. The other is to ensure that our buildings are soundly detailed and as flexible as possible to avoid premature failure or obsolescence. This should avoid the need for early rebuilding, a topic which is considered more fully in Chapter 5, on energy efficiency. Inevitably, there will come a time when even the most durable and flexible building will reach the end of its useful life. Demolition has an environmental dimension as the building type is inextricably linked to the ease of dismantling and the proportion of the fabric which can be recycled. For example, pre-stressed reinforced concrete elements can collapse if the tension in the reinforcement is released in an uncontrolled manner. However, the impact can be reduced by careful thought at the time of original design and construction. Just as new buildings have operating and maintenance manuals, there is no reason why a guide to demolition cannot be issued upon completion to allow easy and safe procedures which maximise recovery of materials for reuse.

6.9 Summary

- There is an environmental dimension to our use of all building materials. The products dealt with in this chapter are some of the main ones, but many principles used apply elsewhere, too.
- The use of tropical hardwoods from non-sustainable sources has a number of environmental consequences. Wherever possible, care should be taken to ensure that tropical hardwoods come from sustainable sources. Where this is not possible, alternative materials can be selected.
- Chlorofluorocarbons contribute to the depletion of the ozone layer and also add to the greenhouse effect. CFCs and associated compounds are found in some insulating materials, fire-extinguishing systems, air-conditioning plant and refrigeration equipment. Their use should be avoided wherever possible, but where they are considered necessary, compounds with the lowest possible ozone-depleting factor should be selected and measures taken to avoid release to the atmosphere.

- As a result of the health risks, asbestos is not generally specified for new work. Where asbestos is discovered in existing buildings, a structured approach should be followed; where encapsulation or removal is appropriate, only suitably licensed contractors should be used.
- There are health implications in the use of solvent-based paints. Water-based paints are being developed and becoming more widely available. Subject to appropriate performance these new products should be used when unacceptable levels of vapour may occur if solvent-based paints are applied.
- Alternatives are available for most uses of toxic lead-based paints and these should be selected.
- Many timber treatments are toxic and therefore their use should be minimised and carefully controlled. An alternative is to obviate the need for timber treatments by careful design and detailing.
- Formaldehyde vapour arising from the use of urea formaldehyde foam insulation in cavity walls can cause a number of harmful symptoms in building occupants. Its use is restricted in new work and remedial action may be necessary where it is found in existing buildings.
- Formaldehyde is also found in some processed timber boards. The cautious approach is to use low-emission boards.
- Recycled or second-hand building components should be considered wherever possible to reduce the environmental impact of building operations.
- Buildings should be soundly detailed using durable materials and be as flexible as possible in order to maximise their useful life. Such an approach implies that the environmental impact of buildings will be minimised because good use will be made of finite materials.
- Our knowledge of the environmental impact of building materials is changing rapidly and there is a need to keep abreast with new products and research.

References

1. Building Research Establishment, *BRE Digest 358 CFCs and Buildings* (Watford: BRE, 1991) p. 2.
2. S. Curwell, C. March and R. Venables (eds), *Buildings and Health – The Rosehaugh Guide to the Design, Construction, Use and Management of Buildings* (London: RIBA Publications, 1990) p. 108.
3. Control of Substances Hazardous to Health Regulations 1988.
4. Health and Safety Commission, *Approved Code of Practice – Safe*

Use of Pesticides for Non-agricultural Purposes (London: HMSO, 1991).

5. Timber Research and Development Association, *Wood Information Section 2/3 Sheet 30* (High Wycombe: TRADA, 1987).
6. Department of the Environment and the Welsh Office, *The Building Regulations 1991, Toxic Substances, Approved Document, D1 Cavity Insulation* (London: HMSO, 1991).
7. National Federation of Building Trades Employers, *Guide to the Use of Urea Formaldehyde Foam Cavity Insulation in New Construction* (London: NFBTE, 1975).
8. Timber Research and Development Association, *TRADA Advisory Sheet 57 Getting Formaldehyde into Perspective* (High Wycombe: TRADA, 1990).
9. The Daily Telegraph and Friends of the Earth, *1990 Directory of Recycling* (London: The Daily Telegraph, 1989) p. 5.

Further reading

Architects' Journal, 'Lead paint – a material analysed', *Architects' Journal* (12 September 1990) pp. 63–5.
Architects' Journal, 'Tropical hardwoods – fruits of the forest', *Architects' Journal* (8 August 1990) pp. 45–52.
Building Research Establishment, *Digest 358 CFCs and Buildings* (Watford: BRE, 1991).
A. H. Cockram and P. J. Arnold, *Information Paper 7/84 Urea Formaldehyde Foam Cavity Wall Insulation: Reducing Formaldehyde Vapour in Dwellings* (Watford: BRE, 1984).
S. Curwell, C. March and R. Venables (eds), *Buildings and Health – The Rosehaugh Guide to the Design, Construction, Use and Management of Buildings* (London: RIBA Publications, 1990).
S. Curwell, S. Fox and C. March, *Use of CFCs in Buildings* (Fernsheer, 1988).
Dulux Trade literature produced by ICI Paints, Slough.
Friends of the Earth, *Good Wood Guide* (London: Friends of the Earth, 1990).
Friends of the Earth, *Good Wood Manual – Specifying Alternatives to Non-renewable Tropical Hardwoods* (London: Friends of the Earth, 1990).
Health & Safety Executive, *Remedial Timber Treatment in Buildings – A Guide to Good Practice and the Safe Use of Wood Preservatives* (London: HMSO, 1991).
R. Lorch, *What Are You Doing About the Environment? The Specifier and Building Materials* (London: Junior Liaison Organisation of the

various professional bodies including the Royal Institute of British Architects, Royal Institution of Chartered Surveyors; etc, 1989).

G. Pleydell, *The Real Wood Guide* (London: Timber Trades Federation, 1990).

Watts & Partners, *Watts & Partners' Handbook 1991* (London: Watts & Partners, 1990).

7 Engineering Services
Andrew Wilkes

7.1 Introduction

Every building has its own internal environmental performance in terms of heat, light and sound. A building may be of low insular rating, such as a greenhouse, or it may be at the opposite extreme, such as a cave. We can see that when the temperature is low outside, the greenhouse quickly reaches the external conditions. Similarly, when it gets dark outside, it gets dark inside. For sound, a noise occurring outside is easily heard inside the greenhouse.

For a cave, the reverse is true. The outside conditions have little or no effect upon the internal environment. Thus, in practice, the greenhouse can be observed as a continually changing internal environment; and a cave, as a very stable situation. The difficulty is that a cave is not particularly habitable for human beings: it is too cold, too damp, too dark and sound reverberates around the hard surfaces. Yet when a fire is lit, thermal comfort is restored; when a light is introduced, visual tasks can be performed; and when fabric is hung on the walls, a more gentle acoustic performance is obtained.

So, engineering systems and services make a cave habitable. Furthermore, in a cave the heat is not wasted to the outside; light can be switched on or off no matter what external light level pervades; and the soft acoustics are much more conducive to conversation. Perhaps the ideal building is a cave? This certainly became the vogue when prime energy costs soared in the mid-1970s when buildings became cave-like in their thermal mass and isolation. We are coming to realise however that human beings, who now spend about 80 per cent of their lives inside buildings of one type or another, lose performance or fall ill when insulated from the outside changing conditions.

Modern buildings require a plethora of building engineering services such as electrical power distribution, telephone and data communications, hot and cold water, lightning protection systems, lifts, escalators, process and medical gases, etc, but environmental engineering services are only part of the picture. Other factors appertaining to the building structure and contents can influence the performance of the internal environment. This holistic approach was highlighted in the recent House of Commons Environment Committee Report into indoor air quality [1].

There is no doubt, however, that the biggest impact upon a building's form and shape is caused by the systems that alter or moderate the internal environment. The other building services systems that purely interface with the user have only to be accommodated within the volume of the building. The categorisation of engineering services into 'environmental engineering' and 'building services' engineering differentiates between these two aspects.

This chapter sets out the various aspects that affect the internal environment and the selection of the most suitable moderating system. In order to understand the contribution that the building form and shape can make, the following section highlights the environmental aspects of the building. Succeeding sections deal with environmental performance; control of personal environments; thermal comfort criteria; ventilation and indoor air quality; and, lastly, factors affecting the selection of heating/ventilating/air-conditioning (or HVAC) systems.

7.2 Environmental aspects of the building

Any building should provide a pleasant and efficient working environment for the occupants of the workspaces. The thermal envelope of the building should be well conceived incorporating glazing solutions that balance fenestration ratios with climatic exposure. Shading of glazed areas should be included to limit the effects of the sun upon the internal environment. It is paramount also to balance any solar shading with the aesthetic appearance of the building exterior. If diminution from total shading is to take place then other measures will have to be introduced to compensate for the higher solar gains.

In the UK, we experience climates that tend not to be extreme – certainly for 80 per cent of the year. Thought processes should be directed, therefore, to only becoming reliant upon an artificially created environment where either the external climate dictates such or the space is remote from naturally obtainable conditioning.

As a generalisation, therefore, buildings should meet the following demands:

- Natural light for the majority of the day.
- An awareness of the outside environmental conditions.

- A changing internal environment which reflects, within limits, the external influences.
- A high quantity of outside air to refresh the internal space.
- A high indoor air quality free of pollutants and dust.
- Insulation in winter.
- Shade in summer.
- Acoustics which ensure privacy.
- Lighting without glare – task lighting where necessary.
- Freer occupation of space and freer control of the environment by occupants.
- Small thermal zones with sensitive controls which respond quickly to comfort requirements.

All these aspects can be created naturally within new buildings and maximised within existing buildings. Unfortunately, the deep-plan, closed-window (or sealed) buildings relying solely on artificial tempering or conditioning are nearly always a 'lost cause' when attempting adequate refurbishment in accord with the aforegoing demands. The overall strategy should be not only to design a building that meets the above demands but also minimises the known causal risk factors.

7.3 Environmental performance

People in naturally ventilated buildings with heating and openable windows will tolerate a wide range of environmental conditions – far from ideal, in fact. The same people in closed-window buildings – when the internal environment is being artificially controlled – will not tolerate even a small drift from the design settings. In some buildings the reaction can be so great that some people find the building environment affects their health detrimentally.

Building operators are experiencing vastly changing expectations regarding the non-visual environment within buildings. The quality of the indoor air that we breathe and the removal of unwanted pollutants from gases emitted by materials used in buildings is only part of the problem. In the same way we have become more aware of additives in food, so our awareness of the impact of the places in which we live and work is increasing – it is no good keeping our minds and bodies fit if we spend the majority of our time in an environment which creates lethargy, lassitude, headaches or upper respiratory tract infections – all symptoms of sick building syndrome.

Sick building syndrome

Environmental psychology, which embraces sick building syndrome, environmental engineering services, lighting, indoor air quality, work-station design, etc, is only part of the synthesis necessary in modern building design and facilities management. The work that Professor Alan Hedge and Andrew Wilkes (the author) undertook at the beginning of the 1980s derived empirical understanding of people's reaction to the buildings in which they worked. They then set about the analysis of this data and examined all the various aspects related to the provision of facilities for people to work.

Hedge and Wilkes quickly came to separate the buildings which were cause for complaint into distinct categories:

- Problem buildings – used to describe any buildings in which the occupants were dissatisfied with their indoor environment.
- Sick buildings – where no single factor could be identified as being the cause, but which nonetheless had a statistical data profile of complaint that impaired the efficiency of the people in the building.

Although in different continents the terminology and main thrust of research is subtly different, people's reactions to the buildings in question have similar frequently occurring symptoms:

- upper respiratory tract infections
- headaches
- lassitude
- lethargy
- runny noses
- sore eyes
- dryness or irritation of the throat
- dry skin

These symptoms are listed in no particular order of importance or occurrence – this aspect is often the most confusing when analysing a building which purports to be 'sick'. As surveys that have been carried out are not comparable it is somewhat difficult to present an order of priority but statistically significant causative parameters can be summarised as follows:

- thermal comfort (temperature and air velocity)
- outside air ventilation rates
- relative humidity

- lighting level, quality, flexibility and glare
- noise from both external and internal sources
- micro-organisms and biocides
- respirable particulates
- volatile organic compounds
- tedious work schedules
- control by occupants
- negative ions
- stress
- musco-skeletal problems
- psycho-social aspects
- response to complaints
- management capability
- poor maintenance regimes

As may be seen and concluded from the foregoing tests, environmental engineering systems dominate sick and problem building causative factors. Professor Alan Hedge at Cornell University, New York [2] has undertaken several studies which have shown major impacts upon three important elements:

- control of personal environmental conditions;
- the number of stressors upon an individual at any one time;
- presence of sub-respirable particles (<0.3 mm) of glass fibre 'sharps'.

Unfortunately, the statistical methods of gathering evidence in a form which readily identifies problem areas within buildings or the population of buildings have been sadly lacking. There is a need to analyse data quickly and present it in concise form. Some bespoke computer-aided tools and programs have been developed but these are not readily available or in a form usable by non-specialists. Computer-aided Facilities Diagnostics (CAFD) [3] programs are, however, becoming more readily available and user-friendly.

No matter what the cause – whether it be subjective, objective or purely psychological – the reduced work performance and increased absenteeism of workers leads to major inefficiency and impaired overall performance of organisations. Some of the foregoing factors relate to organisation or management issues. However, if the building is not planned from the outset to accommodate the intended departmental and individual needs, the manpower efficiency and performance of any organisation will be impaired.

7.4 Control of personal environments

In the early 1980s, Hedge and Wilkes were working upon solutions to the difficulties that occupants suffered in modern closed-window HVAC buildings. They kept coming back to the same role-model much beloved of all studiers of psychology and ego, that of the motor car. Motor car designers had addressed the issue of thermal comfort in most vehicles and there was a definite majority preference for the face-level ventilation to be cooler than the air passing over the occupants' feet and legs.

This 'cool head/warm feet' philosophy was not solely why people were content with the environment of their motor cars (even though internal conditions often varied between extremes of temperature, etc). Another important factor was that people could adjust the temperature, air velocity and direction of the air entering the vehicle – in fact, this adjustment capability almost bordered on 'fidgeting' with the controls when an anxious or stressful situation occurred.

Another major advantage was that passengers and drivers in certain vehicles could have different environmental conditions which further enhanced the overall satisfaction with the comfort of the vehicle. The conclusion drawn from this comparison was that an individual's comfort within buildings might be enhanced by allowing personal selection of environmental conditions.

Further studies showed that personal comfort satisfaction was not purely derived from the ambient conditions in the space but was also affected by such factors as:

- the insulation value of clothing
- gender
- menstrual cycle
- time elapsed from previous meal
- activity level
- well-being and general health

The method of controlling the individual's personal environment was found to be much dependent upon the type of environmental system present and the building's spatial design. For example, if the building had a raised floor to facilitate cable management, air could be introduced into the workstation via the floor void.

Parallel work in Scandinavia, Germany, Canada and the USA tended to tie the environmental systems to the workstation itself, thus introducing conditioned air, etc, via the workstation. The environmental quality in absolute terms is not the overriding criterion in establishing personal satisfaction with comfort levels; it can be argued that the monk working by candle and natural light is equally content as the businessman at his desk in a cellular office. Both have task lighting and control of their own environment.

In a modern open-plan situation, not everyone has the same advantages. Access to natural ventilation and light is very much restricted, and the artificial replacements have been totally misunderstood by the designers, often resorting to such things as task lighting by the selection of a normally ceiling-mounted fixture. Nevertheless, careful design and planning can result in a bright, airy environment which has good personal control.

However, it has been traditional to look at the value of a building in terms of its operational values, namely flexibility and adaptability. This 'value' has an unusual chain of determination:

- designer responds to building developer
- developer responds to institutional standards (fund)
- fund takes advice from letting agents
- letting agents rely on historical data
- historical data does not take into account the productivity value of the building

These criteria often apply even where buildings are custom designed for their occupants. It is therefore important in establishing the total value of the building to consider the productivity values, the thermal environment/comfort, illumination, aesthetics, acoustics and ergonomic furnishing as well as the operational values of flexibility and adaptability. This should not be taken as a substitute for good environmental design, or for basic health considerations such as removal of bacteria, cleanliness of duct-lines, or removal of off-gassing pollutants.

The clear message is that the HVAC designer's responsibilities are vast and all embracing in modern building creation.

7.5 Thermal comfort criteria

Designing to meet reasonable energy targets and to provide satisfactory comfort conditions, particularly at the perimeter of a building in a climate such as the UK, presents a considerable challenge. As a northern European country, the UK is neither hot nor cold in the extreme. The thermal comfort criteria are therefore somewhat distorted compared with a location where air tempering is essential. It is because of this that, in the UK, air conditioning is perceived as being a luxury and of high quality – more often than not leading to acute dissatisfaction from users when conditions are perceived as unacceptable.

The impact of a building upon the people who use it is primarily influenced by the environment in which that person works. The influence of thermal comfort, lighting and noise are the most important aspects to consider. Fresh air ventilation rates and air velocity have a contributory influence and these must not be ignored when attempting to derive an overall solution to meet capital and revenue financial constraints.

From research carried out to date [4], there is fairly strong evidence that a correlation exists between high temperatures and user dissatisfaction within workplaces. Cool environments are regarded as 'fresh' and appear less likely to influence levels of satisfaction with accommodation. Temperature is one of the few parameters that bears a significant contribution to the satisfaction or otherwise of working environments. Winter (heating) comfort conditions are different to summer (cooling) comfort conditions. In winter, temperatures should be limited to 22–3°C whereas 24–5°C is often acceptable in the summer. If temperature alone was the problem, however, then occupants of naturally ventilated, openable window buildings would head the complaint list – it is, in fact, the converse.

Dry bulb air temperature is not the only parameter that should be considered. The ASHRAE Fundamentals [5] F32.7 describes an index known as the effective draught temperature (EDT) which characterises the difference between local and average values of temperature and mean velocity. It is generally accepted that a high percentage of people are comfortable in an office environment if the effective draught temperature is between -1.7 and $+1.1°K$ and the air velocity is less than 0.35 m/s. It is important to ensure a uniformity of such conditions throughout the occupied space and use of the air diffusion performance index (ADPI), which is the percentage of locations which meet the comfort criteria in mechanically ventilated space. An ADPI of at least 70 per cent is the acceptable uniformity that should be aimed for.

Environmental engineering systems should be designed and installed to achieve optimum capital and operating cost commensurate with the maintenance of good environmental conditions in an energy-efficient building.

7.6 Ventilation and indoor air quality

Ventilation is the method whereby the stale air in an internal space is replaced by outside or 'fresh' air. This can be achieved naturally, by opening windows, gaps in construction, ventilators, etc, or by artificial means, such as electric fans, ducts, etc.

The provision of an outside air supply is necessary for the following reasons:

- Human respiration – breathing.
- Dilution and removal of air-borne smells produced within the space.
- Smells include body odours, tobacco smoke, water vapour and 'off-gassing' from products such as glue, cleaning fluids, etc.
- Combustion appliances; boilers.
- Thermal comfort of occupants; the cooling effect of moving air.
- Smoke clearance in the event of a fire.

In Japan and elsewhere some evidence has been found that aroma-therapy principles can be applied to buildings. Consideration has been given to introducing aromatherapy aromas into the building via the HVAC systems. It has already been shown that lemon can energise office workers first thing in the morning; jasmine soothes weary guests; lavender helps to lessen mental fatigue at business meetings; peppermint activates circulatory systems at the gym; and cinnamon piped into a reception area induces calmness. This lateral approach to how air quality affects us is only just being understood.

However, much can be done to alleviate the known problems. So far as ventilation is concerned, this revolves around two aspects: firstly, increase the air quantity and, secondly, locally exhaust the pollutants at source. Both these aspects must be dealt with carefully if operating cost and capital expenditure are to be controlled. International re-search indicates a minimum outside air ventilation rate of 15–17 l/s per person in non-smoking, open-plan spaces. This needs to be increased to 25–30 l/s per person where smoking is allowed. The CIBSE Guide [6] recommendations for the UK and the ASHRAE Standards for the USA have figures lower than these indicators, the fundamental issue of user satisfaction being overlooked in favour of energy considerations alone.

Any new building should have a high allowance for outside air ventilation. A combination of natural ventilation using openable win-dows and artificial ventilation using ducted air will ensure that flexi-bility is inherent in the basic design. As many of the windows as possible should be openable which will have the benefit of enabling the building to function without the full HVAC system being opera-tional – a situation frequently occurring in the UK but little utilised.

Building management systems

An advanced building management system (ABMS) could be designed to instruct the centralised outside air plant to 'purge' the building during the non-occupied periods if the outside ambient conditions are suitable. Contaminants are not effectively removed from a building unless high fresh air ventilation rates are present. A considerable amount of research work has been undertaken into buildings which introduce fresh air purging during unoccupied periods at night. This principle has resulted in increased performance from office workers and a greater feeling of well-being due to the freshening of the internal environment.

The concentration of pollutants in the occupied zones should be considered. This is best achieved by utilising a displacement ventilation principle – supplying air at floor level and at low velocity. However, practical and aesthetic considerations may discount the use of true displacement ventilation. Nevertheless, by extracting air at a high level, it is possible to remove the higher concentrations of pollutants.

Studies of human activity show that the typical Western person now spends over 80 per cent of his life breathing the air inside buildings of one form or another, e.g. homes, schools, offices, hospitals, and yet, to date, relatively little attention has been focused on defining what constitutes a healthy indoor atmosphere.

Studies of unsatisfactory indoor air quality have not identified polluted outdoor air as the problem source. Perhaps an example of an exception to this is in office buildings where garage-generated pollutants from underground car parking can infiltrate the indoor air of the office. Indeed, many of the air pollutants of concern to occupants of office buildings are generated inside the building itself. Typical indoor sources include the occupants and their activities; office technology; materials and furnishings; and the ventilation system duct lines and equipment.

People occupying a space continuously emit at least four types of pollutants: carbon dioxide (CO_2), particles, body odours and micro-organisms. Traditionally, health ventilation standards were designed to reduce levels of CO_2 and body odours to acceptable limits. The production of these pollutants depends on the number of occupants in a space and their metabolic activity levels, as well as the amount of ventilation of that space.

What people do inside an office and what kinds of equipment they use can affect the types of indoor air pollutants released into that space. People smoking indoors release a complex array of substances into the air. Devices such as photocopiers, diazo copiers, litho-offset printers or simply the use of correction fluids or solvents all lead to the generation of indoor air pollutants.

The types of materials used either to construct or finish an office can affect indoor pollution levels. For example, the type of floor covering and adhesives used may add appreciable amounts of certain pollutants to indoor air, as can furnishings and decorations such as painted surfaces.

It has been suggested that a CO_2 concentration of greater than 600 ppm may result in increased discomfort for occupants. While it is true that CO_2 generated indoors can be reduced by increasing building ventilation it does not seem to be the case that other air pollutants necessarily respond in the same manner to increased ventilation. Indeed, CO_2 is the only pollutant to decrease significantly with increased fresh air ventilation – carbon monoxide, hydrocarbons and particulates all maintain steady levels irrespective of ventilation. Pollutants respond differently to ventilation. No one pollutant can serve as a predictor of total air quality.

In response to the need to remove pollutants by filtration rather than ventilation, a concept has been developed called 'breathing zone filtration' (BZF) [7]. This concept has already received wide acclaim and acceptance not only by users but also by furniture system manufacturers who incorporate such filters into workstation arrangements. The creation of an 'umbrella' of HEPA (high efficiency particulate air) filter-cleaned air surrounds the occupants resulting in better well-being and lower absenteeism – due to the lack of cross-contamination of adjacent workers. Although highly effective, the concept is neither expensive nor wasteful in energy and worthy of consideration for new and refurbished situations.

7.7 Heating/ventilating/air-conditioning (HVAC) systems

Any building concept can accommodate a HVAC system that generally matches the expectations of modern building users. However, the physical size of the HVAC system depends upon the thermal loads within the building that have to be treated. In winter, if the insulation of the building is too low, a very large boiler/pipework requirement exists. Similarly, in summer, if the solar gain is not properly controlled, very large cooling plant is required.

As has been emphasised earlier in this chapter, the modern approach to 'responsible buildings' is to eliminate the need for high energy use (see also Chapter 5, on energy efficiency). In addition, the current environmental concerns regarding ozone layer depletion and global warming need highlighting.

Chlorofluorocarbons

Work in developing environmentally acceptable alternatives for fully halogenated chlorofluorocarbons (CFCs) has been much slower than was originally anticipated. The shortening of phase-out programmes announced by most countries has created problems for manufacturers and specifiers alike. In existing installations, 'drop-in' refrigerants have been sought whereby compatibility is the overriding driving force. The original choice of R11 and R12 compounds was because they were non-toxic and highly efficient. Replacements have to date been inefficient, flammable or toxic.

In new buildings, much more flexibility is available in meeting cooling requirements. Oversizing of equipment to compensate for low-efficiency refrigerants is frequently occurring, but the direction demanded by responsible buildings is not to just reduce environmental impact but to minimise or remove altogether the offending products. The probability of negating the need for air conditioning is very high for UK-based buildings, thus removing the need for chemical refrigerants. In the event that CFC refrigerants are required, information on their performance and the availability of substitutes is set out in BRE Digest 358 [8].

A similar argument applies to greenhouse warming gases. By making the building more efficient, the need to input high energy is minimised, resulting in lower spent-fuel gas emissions. Attention is drawn to Chapter 5, on energy efficiency, where the need for efficient building envelopes, services and controls is set out.

Legionnaires' disease

A final comment at this juncture relates to the effects of legionnaires' disease. Heat rejection from refrigeration systems for air conditioning falls into two categories: air-to-air and air-to-water systems. Air-to-air systems tend to take up more space and are, in general, more expensive. Air-to-water systems are correspondingly more compact and have a cheaper capital cost. However, poorly maintained water system 'cooling towers' have been responsible for the spread of *Legionella pneumophilia* bacterium.

Well maintained 'wet' systems are, in fact, not a problem. Although easily monitored regimes can be put in place, there is a general reluctance to select such 'wet' systems following the safe option of air-cooled condensers. This reluctance should be scrutinised to avoid premature abandonment of viable solutions.

General considerations

The impact upon the building of the HVAC system affects the following aspects:

- Energy use of the building and maintenance costs.
- Plant space to be accommodated both centrally (in a basement or on a roof) and decentrally (around the building).
- Vertical ductwork and pipework space (the larger the thermal load, the larger the ducts and pipes) and the impact of such large items upon the aesthetic proportion of the external elevations.
- Horizontal ductwork and pipework space. In this aspect, if the building has too high a thermal load then the service zones have to be deeper and the height of the building increased. If the site has a height restriction, this would mean the loss of occupied floor space.
- The selection of the most suitable HVAC system. Many systems cannot handle the largest of the thermal loads or are inefficient when high thermal loads exist. Conversely, some systems are incapable of operating effectively where the thermal load varies widely.

The first objective must be to design a building which minimises the need for mechanical HVAC treatment. The necessity of considering a highly efficient glazing system together with solar shading are paramount in the selection of the most suitable HVAC system. The following comments are based upon the assumption that a good thermal performance exists on the envelope of the building. Given the climatic conditions of the UK, the expectations of the users and the current/ future office technology, it is necessary to consider carefully any artificially controlled environment.

HVAC systems must address the following:

- maximum usable/lettable floor spaces
- maximum space flexibility
- lowest operating costs and energy usage
- comfortable working environments
- compatibility with aesthetic requirements
- acceptable sound levels and acoustic performance
- durability of equipment in use
- ease of maintenance without undue operating disruption
- localised control options creating small central zones – individual control if possible
- minimised service zone depth and plantroom volumes

- horizontal and vertical duct/pipe run accommodation
- sill height of windows
- electrical distribution complexity and loads
- water pipework distribution complexity
- ductwork distribution complexity
- reduction in CFC load
- avoiding legionnaires' disease

There are approximately 20 recognised types of air-conditioning system used around the world on a regular basis. There are as many again which are variations on a theme and are less widely used because they have major disadvantages or are specific to various uses, for example computer suites. No single air-conditioning system is best for all buildings or all climates. Opinions vary widely on which is the best type of system, with promoters often trying to generalise to prove specific points.

There are primarily two ways of distributing warmth or coolth [9] around a building: by air or by a liquid. Air is not a particularly good thermal conductor but it is the medium in which we live and breathe. Therefore, whatever concept is chosen, the final distribution of warmth or coolth uses air movement. However, returning to the aspect of thermal efficiency, in order to transport a given quantity of warmth or coolth, a larger volume of air is required than liquid. Thus, in general terms, air-to-air systems require much larger ducts than liquid-to-air systems which use small diameter pipes to carry the liquid.

Another factor is that it is normal for large-scale energy creation/exchange to be more efficient than smaller scale examples – for example, electricity power stations, district heating schemes, etc. In the same way, heating by centralised boilers or cooling by centralised chillers is more economic in use than decentralised equipment.

In any building, the use of a centralised system – whereby air is used to distribute the warmth/coolth – as opposed to a decentralised system has the following implications:

- Centralised plant space on either the roof or in the basement would be larger for a centralised system.
- Horizontal space for ducts would be deeper for a centralised system.
- Vertical space for ducts would be larger for a centralised system.

The major trade-offs of a centralised system to these impositions are:

- lower energy costs
- lower maintenance costs

- longer life expectancy of dynamic equipment
- substantially less intrusion into occupied spaces during maintenance

The two main principles for centralised systems are:

- constant volume, variable temperature (CAV)
- variable volume, constant temperature (VAV)

Both these principles have advantages over each other and both have specific applications which are most appropriate.

VAV undoubtedly offers major savings in energy due to the turn-down ratio which effectively varies the volume of air depending upon what thermal load is present in the space. However, in perimeter zones and especially in heating periods, the reduction in air can often lead to poor air distribution and a resulting down-draught from glazing. To overcome this, perimeter heating systems need to be introduced to counteract the effect in winter. The problem can also be acute in summer, cooling, conditions when the asymmetric radiation from glazing is quite high. The solution is to introduce perimeter conditioning which has a constant volume component that is variable in temperature to cope with the localised condition and a variable volume component to handle the occupational thermal loads.

Thus, it can be immediately seen that there are variations of VAV which should be considered at the conceptual design stage. It should be anticipated that an advanced building management system would be used and the powerful control regime that this allows is advantageous when selecting a sophisticated VAV system.

Such possibilities are:

- Variable volume and temperature (VVT) whereby local control can be introduced to reschedule the individual zone-mixing box by addressing a central microprocessor-based controller.
- Fan-assisted terminal VAV (FATVAV) whereby the low-volume, poor-air distribution problems are overcome by recirculating local air through the VAV mixing box with the turned-down incoming air.

Whilst addressing the fundamental principles of a HVAC system, the overall energy usage has to be considered. There are several additional techniques that have recently been developed to assist in reducing energy costs further. The first has been commented upon previously in this chapter and relates to introducing the cooler night-time air into the building when the night air temperature is lower. This concept is called 'night-time purging' because the whole system turns over to 100 per cent full outside air ventilation. A major by-product of this temperature control concept is that unwanted pollutants, odours, etc, are removed at the same time while a fresher, healthier environment is reported by occupants when they enter the building the following morning. This concept has similarity to opening all the windows after a party to let out all the smoke and smells. The second technique involves the storage of warmth or coolth at times when energy costs are less expensive and reintroducing the warmth/coolth when the building demands it. This technique is properly termed 'thermal storage', but is often referred to as 'ice storage'.

The argument for thermal storage revolves around the availability of cheap night-time electricity. However, special considerations such as examination of a full-year's thermal conditions need to be carried out if the optimum sizing of plant is taken into account. Such an example is where a building has a peak duty of, say, 400 kW. This is normally the criterion used for the selection of plant. Yet the April or October peak duty may well be less than 100 kW and the plant underutilised. These misconceptions result in equipment running inefficiently for the majority of the year in addition to the initial capital cost excesses.

What stems from this comment is that a complex analysis needs to take place on the building to ascertain whether thermal storage is an economic viability or not. It is now clear that if the size of the plant can be reduced, then the amount of refrigerant employed can be similarly reduced *pro rata*. Smaller plants are able to use ozone-friendly refrigerants. Thus, the use of thermal storage has many attractions beyond the immediate energy considerations. An additional factor relates to the overall HVAC system constraints. Low-temperature (7°C ± 1°C) air distribution combined with thermal storage can reduce capital costs, electricity demand and, in some cases, plant space in the building where smaller equipment can be utilised.

All these refined systems have major individual advantages yet to achieve the maximum benefit, complex thermal load pattern analysis needs to be carried out. Furthermore, the advanced building management system must have a user-friendly interface which allows easy and frequent fine-tuning by facilities managers to optimise the very complex dynamics of the combined systems.

The purpose of this chapter has not been to create an absolute reference work on the complex technical and practical aspects of HVAC design. A much more detailed explanation is given in such books as the classic *Heating and Air Conditioning of Buildings* by Faber and Kell [10].

7.8 Summary

- The Industrial Revolution dramatically changed the manner in which buildings affected the human body. We have solved most of the fatal effects but we have yet to properly address and to solve the effects that reduce performance or impair well-being.
- Employee costs are now so significant that inefficiencies have a major impact upon the profitability and competitiveness of organisations.
- Internal environmental conditioning can be naturally or artificially created. The demands upon modern buildings from users and office equipment require substantial environmental and building services systems. The systems dramatically affect the form and shape of structures.
- If a building can be designed with the impact of external influences as well as internal influences being controlled, the environmental systems can be minimised.
- In addition to air quality and quantity issues, the ability of building users to relate to outside conditions and to control their own personal environments has a marked effect upon well-being and satisfaction.
- The selection of heating, ventilation and air-conditioning (HVAC) systems is a major contributory factor when attempting to create thermal comfort and minimise the way in which buildings impact on the human body.
- The future success of any modern building will therefore depend upon a whole range of influencing factors that are the domain of the environmental and building services engineer. A new breed of such engineers is creating solutions to match the future expectations – that of responsible buildings.

References

1. House of Commons Environment Committee, *Sixth Report into Indoor Pollution*, Volumes I & II (London: HMSO, June 1991).
2. House of Commons Environment Committee, Appendix 23, *The 'Sick' Building Syndrome in Offices*, to House of Commons Environment Committee Sixth Report into Indoor Pollution, Volume II, pp. 355–9 (London: HMSO, June 1991).
3. House of Commons Environment Committee, Appendix 35, *Recommendations for Managing Indoor Air Quality Complaints in Buildings*, to House of Commons Environment Committee Sixth

Report into Indoor Pollution, Volume II, pp. 416–25 (London: HMSO, June 1991).

4. I. N. Potter, *The Sick Building Syndrome – Symptoms, Risk Factors and Practical Design Guidance* (Building Services Research and Information Association (BSRIA), Technical Note 4/88).

5. American Society of Heating, Refrigerating and Air-Conditioning Engineers Inc, Publications Sales Department, 1791 Tullie Circle, NE, Atlanta, GA 30329, USA.

6. Chartered Institution of Building Services Engineers, Delta House, 222 Balham High Road, London SW12 9BS.

7. *Energy Efficient Alternatives to Additional Dilution Ventilation: The Effects of Breathing-zone Filtration on IAQ.* Section 6.0 of a statement presented to the New York State Assembly in support of State Government Policy for Diagnosing and Managing Indoor Air Quality and Sick Building Syndrome Complaints in Buildings by Professor Alan Hedge (New York State, January 1991).

8. Building Research Establishment, *Digest 358 CFCs and Buildings* (Watford: BRE, 1991).

9. The term 'coolth' is defined in *Webster's Third New International Dictionary* (unabridged) as – coolth (cool plus -th (as in warmth)): the state or occasion of being cool.

10. Faber and Keller, *Heating and Air-conditioning of Buildings*, 6th revised edition by J. R. Kell and P. L. Martin (Essex: Butterworth Architecture, 1988).

Further reading

Air-Conditioning Systems for Commercial Buildings, Carrier Distribution Ltd, Carrier House, The Crescent, Leatherhead, Surrey KT22 8DY.

A J Guide to Space for Services, Architect's Journal Reprint (London, 1986).

Reyner Balham, *The Architecture of the Well-tempered Environment*, 2nd edition (London: The Architectural Press, 1984).

Nigel Dudley, *Good Health on a Polluted Plant* (Chatham, Kent: Thornsons, 1991).

Duffy, Cave and Worthington, *The Planning Office Space* (Bradford-upon-Avon, Wiltshire: Butterworth Architecture, 1988).

8 Building Biology and Health
Jagjit Singh

8.1 Introduction

Building biology deals with the study of living organisms in and around the building environment which have direct and indirect effect on the health of the building fabric, its materials, structures, environments and occupants. Building structures and environments provide specialised micro-climates and ecological niches in their ecosystems for the settlement, growth and proliferation of a variety of living organisms. These biological agents can cause damage to the building structure, decorations and contents and can raise concerns for the indoor air quality and the health of the building occupants.

The impact of building biology on the biodeterioration of building structures, contents, materials and decorations is man's commonest problem and it can be traced back to biblical times or earlier. The estimated cost of repairing damage caused by biological agents in buildings in the UK is £400 million a year. These biological agents have not only a serious impact on the maintenance and repair of the national housing stock but also cause great concern regarding the conservation of ancient and historic buildings and buildings of special architectural and cultural merit including their contents and decorations. The most common biological agents which trigger biodeterioration in buildings include fungi and insects. For example, the most destructive fungal species which cause the decay of structural timber in buildings are dry rot (*Serpula lacrymans*), wet rot (*Coniophora puteana*) and a number of other wet rot, soft rot and surface rot fungi and moulds. Among the many insects found in buildings, beetles are the most dangerous, causing serious damage to timbers. Deathwatch beetle (*Xestobium rufovillosum*) and the common furniture beetle (*Anobium punctatum*) are extremely destructive insects.

People spend long periods indoors, and both at home and at work the air that they breathe is mostly indoor air. Health and comfort problems associated with the indoor climate have come to constitute a

122

major problem in recent years. The main reason for the neglect of indoor air quality issues was the lack of awareness of the problem because the effects are mostly chronic and long term and are not directly and immediately life threatening. The main biological factors causing building-related sickness are mould, fungi, bacteria, viruses, protozoa, pollens, house dust mites, insect pests, algae, pigeons and rodents. For some people, an allergic reaction may be triggered by non-biological factors such as chemicals and other indoor air pollutants or emotional stress, fatigue and changes in the weather. These factors burden allergic people further if they are suffering from allergic reactions to biological contaminants. This combination is known as 'the allergic load'. There are a number of environmental, design, use, management and construction factors which influence allergic components, for example geographical location, time of year, time of day, altitude, weather conditions, flora and fauna, shape and configuration, materials and structures, design of ventilation systems, thermal insulation, tightness, air change and energy. At present, there are no government guidelines or code of practice on indoor air quality which specifically identify exposure limits for an extended list of pollutants based on possible total exposure (ambient, home and workplace).

Orthodox remedial measures to control biological agents, including the use of chemicals, not only cause concern to health authorities and environmentalists but develop resistance in target organisms and can result in the loss of irreplaceable decorative finishes. For these reasons, fundamental scientific knowledge of these organisms together with a multi-disciplinary scientific knowledge of building construction and environment is preferred. These investigations can provide more effective, economical and less destructive environmental control strategies.

8.2 Building environments

Buildings can be likened to living organisms. The useful life of a building depends on its internal and external environments, both in terms of longevity of materials and as an appropriate habitat for its occupants. Buildings work as spatial environmental ecosystems and provide ecological niches and micro-climates for wide varieties of biological lives and must be understood as a whole. The interrelationships of building structures and materials with their environments and the living organisms within them are very complex. These interrelationships must be analysed through a multi-disciplinary scientific study of buildings in order to improve the role of the building environment from a total health perspective.

Buildings separate their occupants from hostile external environments and create a better internal environment for them. Therefore, buildings can be likened to human skin (a second skin) or an extension of our bodies as the third skin, that is, the body is the first skin and clothes are the second skin, which forms a physical barrier to separate the inside from the outside [1, 2].

The building shell needs to be adaptive, flexible and reactive in order to maintain a relatively constant building environment in circumstances of regular or cyclical changing external conditions and the varying activities of the occupants. Changing internal environments and their effect on the fabric and contents of the building, both fully controlled 'museum' environments and simpler and more intermittently operated systems, must be understood as a whole. These changes can be permanent radical changes; for example, the installation of a new heating system; shifting equilibrium, a progressive change from one state to another; spatial variations, non-uniform environments which result from diverse occupancy, both in space and time; cyclic fluctuations, the control strategies of most heating and ventilation systems; seasonal variations; and violent changes [3]. The house must function in close correspondence with the processes and biorhythms of the body, for example regulation of moisture, breathing and heat balance. These issues have led us to understand the need for the use of ecologically sound materials to design a breathing fabric.

Building investigators have failed to diagnose problems in buildings because they have not approached the buildings as a dynamic complex system. Most commonly, building failure leads to biological decay problems being dealt with by drastic measures, rather than a comprehensive multi-disciplinary approach. The causes of decay in materials and structures and the effect on the health of the occupants are influenced by the internal building environment which has a varied micro-climate depending upon the structural aspects. The environment of a material is complex and dynamic. All organisms live in a biological equilibrium called 'biological balance' and for an organism to succeed it must be in balance within fine limits with the environment [4]. Similarly, the internal building environment is a complicated interacting system comprising moisture movements from moisture sources through moisture reservoirs to moisture sinks, air movement and the transfer of heat, and the ways in which a building modifies the external environmental conditions to create an internal environment. The internal building environment is specific to each building depending upon its design, construction, materials, thermal mass, buffer effect and insulation, and also upon its maintenance condition and usage, as well as its acoustics, lighting, heating and ventilation. An imprudent alteration of the internal environment may upset a very delicate, long established equilibrium.

The environmental factors that cause building failures and favour the decay of building structures, contents and decorations are temperature, water, humidity and lack of ventilation. Serious moisture damage in buildings is usually the result of a combination of unfortunate circumstances, general neglect, bad maintenance and design flaws [5]. Studies on moisture profiles in walls have shown that occasional condensation does not give rise to biological problems, hence it does not damage the structure or the materials.

8.3 Biological decay

The following organisms are among the most important which affect building structures, materials, contents and decorations.

Dry rot (Serpula lacrymans)

In Britain, the term 'dry rot' refers to a type of timber decay in buildings caused by the true dry rot fungus *Serpula lacrymans* (formerly known as *Merulius lacrymans*). Dry rot fungus attacks mostly softwood and often causes extensive damage [6]. The term dry rot is rather misleading, as moist conditions are required to initiate the growth in timber (a moisture content of about 20 to 30 per cent) and optimum growth is continued at about 20 per cent. Spore germination requires a more precisely favourable micro-climate at the wood surface. The fungus has the ability to grow through plaster, brickwork and masonry and even extends a distance of several metres from its food source to attack sound timber using specialised hyphal strands (rhizomorphs). Rhizomorphs are conducting strands formed by the mycelium and they are able to transport nutrients and water. Rhizomorphs may be up to 6 mm in diameter. They are relatively brittle when dry. These adaptations to the building environment make it one of the fungi which causes most rapid decay and it is probably the most difficult to control. Conditions of static dampness are particularly favourable to *S. lacrymans*; unlike wet rot fungi, it is able to tolerate fluctuating conditions. Active growth is indicated by silky white sheets or cotton wool-like white cushions with patches of lemon yellow or lilac tinges when exposed to light, perhaps covered with tears or water drops in unventilated conditions. This exudation of water is the way the fungus relates the atmospheric relative humidity and is the explanation for the latin name 'lacrymans'.

Figure 8.1   Dry rot fruiting body.

Mycelial strands are white to grey and are often subsequently green in colour through developments of superficial saprophytic mould growth.

Sporophores or fruiting bodies generally develop under unfavourable temperature and humidity conditions and as a result of exhausting its supply of nutrients. The sporophores are tough, fleshy, pancake and bracket shaped, varying from an inch (25 mm) to a yard (a metre) or more across (Figure 8.1). The centre is yellow-ochre coloured when young, darkening to rusty red when mature, owing to spore production. The fruiting body is covered with shallow pores or folds and the margin is white and grey. The appearance of the fruiting body together with a distinctive 'mushroom' odour, may be, and usually is, the first indication of an outbreak of dry rot, as fungal growth in buildings is generally concealed.

Wood thoroughly rotted by the dry rot fungus, *S. lacrymans*, is light in weight, crumbles under the fingers, is a dull brown colour and has lost its fresh resinous smell. Wood damaged by this fungus shows a typical cubical cracking along and across the grain. Dry rot is also called brown rot, a term relating to the manner in which it destroys the cellulose but leaves the lignin largely unaltered so that the wood acquires a distinctive brown colour and its structural strength is almost entirely lost.

Wet rot

Wet rot is caused by a number of Basidiomycetes fungi of which the most important are *Coniophora puteana* (cerebella), 'Poria' fungi, *Phellinus contiguus*, *Donkiporia expansa*, *Pleurotus ostreatus*, *Asterostroma* spp and *Paxillus panuoides*. Wet rot is also called white rot as it destroys both cellulose and lignin, leaving the colour of the wood largely unaltered but producing a soft felty or spongy texture without cross cracks. Common white rots are *Donkiporia expansa*, *Asterostroma* spp, *Pleurotus ostreatus* and *Phellinus contiguus*. Brown rots cause the wood to become darker in colour and to crack along and across the grain; when dry, very decayed wood crumbles to dust. Many common wet rots are brown rots, for example *Coniophora puteana*, *C. marmorata*, *Paxillus panuoides* and *Dacrymyces stillatus*.

Cellar rot fungus – *Coniophora puteana* and *C. marmorata* – is the most common cause of wet rot in buildings which have become soaked by water leakage, for example soil moisture or plumbing leaks. The hyphae are initially white, then yellow to brownish in colour, remaining off-white under impervious coverings (Figure 8.2). *C. puteana* forms rhizomorphs that are initially yellowish when young, becoming brown to black at maturity. They never extend from the infected wood. The sporophore rarely occurs in buildings and consists of an olive green to brown fruit body with a paler margin, thin skin and warty surface [7]. The *C. marmorata* fruit body is pinkish brown and has a smooth to lumpy surface.

The fungus causes considerable shrinkage to wood, and cracking may occur, not unlike that caused by dry rot. The rotted wood is dark brown with dominant longitudinal cracks and infrequent cross-grain cracks. Freshly colonised wood usually shows a yellow colouration.

Soft rot

Soft rot is as prevalent as other rots, but it is less damaging and less detectable. Soft rot can be regarded as a superficial form of wet rot. It is more usually found in timber in ground contact. The most destructive of the species is *Chaetomium globosum*. Soft rot fungi are capable

Figure 8.2   Cellar rot fungus.

of enduring the micro-climate of wood surfaces, that is, they can tolerate higher temperatures, higher pHs and even grow in restricted oxygen (Cartwright and Findlay 1954).

Hardwoods are more susceptible to soft rot than are softwoods. It is mostly the outer wood which is severely damaged by soft rot. As revealed by probing with a knife, the conspicuously degraded wood may be comparatively shallow and the transition between it and the underlying firm wood may be quite abrupt. When wet, the wood may be so decomposed that it can be scraped from the surface with a finger nail. When dry, the surface appears as though it has been lightly charred, and there will be profuse fine cracking and fissuring both with and across the grain [8]. Soft rot is mainly associated with waterlogged wood; quays, jetties, mills and boathouses may have affected wood components.

Moulds

The great majority of moulds which are found in buildings belong to the class Hyphomycetes of the subdivision Deuteromycotina. They live mainly on starch and free sugars stored in parenchyma or surface deposits of detritus on masonry, brickwork, concrete, rendering, tiles and paving, and on the surfaces of damp wood, plaster, wallpaper or paint. Moulds commonly occur on surfaces as a superficial growth, causing patchy surface discolouration, usually green, grey, or black,

Figure 8.3   Mould growth in buildings.

occasionally pink or yellow (Figure 8.3). Some are rusty red and may be mistaken for the spores of *S. lacrymans*, whilst others produce a fluffy mass of white growth. Some moulds colonise wood whose moisture content is above 20 per cent.

Moulds cause some loss in wood toughness (resistance of shock) but usually have only a negligible effect on other strength values. They discolour and seriously weaken such materials as paper, leather, cloth, and fibre-based products such as acoustic tiles, insulation, etc. Moulds greatly increase the porosity of wood, and mouldy wood wets much more easily, thus increasing the likelihood of decay and moisture-induced deformations. The presence of actively growing moulds serves as an indication that a moisture problem exists, which may or may not present a potential decay hazard.

Common moulds in buildings are: *Cladosporium* spp, *Penicillium* spp, *Aspergillus* spp, *Trichoderma viride* and *Alternaria* spp.

Slime moulds

Slime moulds belong to the division Myxomycota due to the presence of plasmodium. Myxomycetes are very common on fallen tree trunks and branches. In buildings they are usually found on inorganic substrates such as masonry, brickwork, concrete, rendering, tiles, paving and organic substances, such as damp wood, usually exterior joinery.

Figure 8.4   Peziza *growth on buildings.*

Plaster fungi

These fungi are likely to be found on damp brickwork or plaster in buildings (Figure 8.4). Common examples are *Coprinus* spp (Inkcap), *Peziza* spp (Elf Cup) and *Pyronema domesticum*. These fungi feed on surface detritus or on organic material found in walls, such as bituminised felt dpcs and hair contained in old plasters.

Stain fungi

Staining of sapwood is usually blue to black, occurring on freshly felled wood with a high moisture content. The damage persists after the wood dries, but is usually of no significance when found in wood in buildings. Stain fungi cannot grow in waterlogged wood or below a moisture content of about 20 per cent.

Stain fungi commonly harbour sapwood cells of moist wood but consist mainly of ray cells. For their early nourishment they depend on parenchymatous tissues as in the wood rays, and on sugars and starch in the cells. The virtual absence of blue stain fungi in heartwood seems to be attributable chiefly to a shortage of relatively easily metabolised carbohydrates rather than inhibitory heartwood activities. Stain fungi are also commonly called 'sap stain', a blue stain.

Stain fungi commonly found in buildings are *Aureobasidium pullulans* and *Sclerophoma pithyophila*, most of them belonging to the class Hypomycetes of the subdivision Deuteromycotina. Some stain fungi, for example *Ceratocystis* spp, belong to the subdivision Ascomycotina.

Stains are troublesome due to their objectionable appearance and disfigurement of the wood, especially of clear finishes; early failure of surfaces may be brought about by rupture caused by the fruit bodies. Discoloration caused by sap stain which has occurred in the log may still be detectable after the drying and conversion of the timber but this will affect only the aesthetic value of the wood. Damage of the coatings will occur only through the growth of blue stain in service.

Bacteria

Bacteria cause damage to both timber and stone in buildings. They colonise water-saturated wood, since they require very low amounts of free oxygen for growth or they can thrive under nearly anaerobic conditions. Bacteria initially colonise the parenchyma cells of wood rays and resin ducts. However, as the readily available carbohydrates stored in these cells are depleted, the pit membranes and, later, walls of trachieds, fibres and vessels are attacked and degraded. This causes a slow progressive loss in wood strength and an increase in the permeability of the wood which adds to the chance of seasonal rain wetting, thus increasing the risk of decay. Bacteria, like rotters and moulds, can detoxify creosote and have shown a high tolerance to copper-chrome-arsenic, pentachlorophenol and tributyltin oxide.

Bacteria are also important contributors to paint film deterioration; for example, *Flavobacterium marinum* is the major contributor to the disfigurement or deterioration of paint films.

Stone deterioration is caused by various bacteria, e.g. sulphating bacteria, *Thiobacillus* spp, nitrating bacteria, *Nitrobacter* spp and sewerage bacteria, *Desulphovibrio* spp.

Many species of bacteria occur in wood, depending upon the microclimate at the wood surface. However, species of Bacillus, Aerobacter and Pseudomonas are the most common.

Actinomycetes

Little attention has been paid to the role of Actinomycetes in the biodeterioration of wood in comparison to fungi and bacteria. However, frequent isolation of Actinomycetes in ecological studies from wood stored in a variety of natural environments and the association of

Actinomycetes with preservative-treated wood have encouraged a greater interest in this group of micro-organisms [9].

The major species of cellulolytic Actinomycetes are *Streptomyces* spp, *Nocardia* spp and *Micromonosphore* spp. However, their importance in the biodeterioration of timber in buildings is not fully studied. They tend to be overlooked in conventional wood isolation studies or are simply described as bacteria due to the difficulties in identifying them to species level. Furthermore, their taxonomy is still unclear.

Lichens, mosses and algae

Lichens, mosses and algae cause a chemical dissimilatory type of biodeterioration. They grow upon, rather than within, various building materials and use them primarily for support and as a source of moisture. Damage caused by such plants is usually confined to the surface discoloration of wood, concrete, brick, asbestos-cement and asphaltic materials.

Lichens are compound organisms, consisting of algae and fungi in symbiotic association. The fungal hyphae penetrate into the stone by exploring cracks and crannies, and also by generating organic acids such as oxalic acid. These acids dissolve the stone material which is usually redeposited as calcium oxalate close to the thallus. Acids produced by lichens and mosses do not only damage carbonaceous stones such as limestones or sandstones with a carbonate cementing matrix but will also attack silica and cause etching damage on granite and even glass surfaces. When these occur on roof slopes the acid can cause very severe deterioration of metal gutters. The lichens of *Calaplaca* spp are usually associated with limestones, whilst *Tecidea* and *Rhizocarpa* spp are usually associated with sandstones.

The growth of algae, lichens and mosses usually indicates a high moisture content – they can be used as biological indicators of water levels and potential wood decay problems in wooden structures. Their presence also increases the likelihood of wood being colonised by fungi, because their growth inhibits wood drying and dead plant cells provide additional nutrients for fungi, such as *Aspergillus* spp, *Cladosporium* spp, *Penicillium* spp, *Aureobasidium* spp and *Alternaria* spp. These accumulating deposits also permit higher plants to develop, particularly grasses.

Insects

Many kinds of insect are found in buildings, for instance, casual visitors, such as bees, wasps, earwigs, snails, commensal insects, cock-

Figure 8.5   Woodworm on wood.

roaches and insects associated with the structure of buildings, for example with built-in timber. Most of the wood-boring insects will attack only damp wood or are encouraged by dampness, while some have a preference for wood which is already partly pre-digested by fungal attack. The two main destructive insects in this group are described below.

Woodworm *(Anobium punctatum)*

This is by far the most widespread wood-destroying beetle in Britain. It is also called the common furniture beetle. It attacks mainly softwoods and European hardwoods and is found in structural timbers and in older furniture; it can also attack panel products with animal-based adhesives.

Infestation is usually detected by emergence holes and tunnels which are up to 1 to 2 mm in diameter, circular and mainly in the direction of the grain (Figure 8.5). The frass produced in the holes is cream coloured and contains lemon-shaped pellets. It is gritty when rubbed between the fingers. The adult insect is not visible for most of its life cycle and is usually 3 to 5 mm long and dull brown in colour.

Deathwatch beetle *(Xestobium rufovillosum)*

This is a pest of hardwoods such as oak or elm used structurally in historic buildings; it also attacks softwoods, particularly when in contact with infested hardwood and other hardwoods which have been affected by a fungus. Larvae continue to burrow slowly through sound oak wood for 10 to 12 years without any sign of pupation, but if the oak has been partially decayed by a wood-rotting fungus, pupation can occur after about two years and the adult beetles emerge three years after egg laying.

Emergence holes and tunnels are circular, 3 mm in diameter and are extensive mainly in the direction of the grain of the wood. The frass is cream coloured while the pellets are disc shaped and gritty when rubbed between the fingers (Richardson 1980).

The other common species in buildings are: powder post beetles (*Lyctus* spp), house longhorn beetle (*Hylotropes bajulus*), wood-boring weevils (*Pentarthrum huttoni* and *Euophryum confine*), Ptilinus beetle (*Ptilinus pectinicornis*), wharf borer beetle (*Nacerdes melanura*), Tenebrionid beetle (*Tenebrio mollitor*), leaf cutter bees (*Megachile* spp) and solitary wasp (*Crabro* spp) (BRE 1987).

Termites

Termites are essentially a problem of tropical and subtropical regions. They are not a problem in the UK; however, they are also a limited hazard to wood in service in some temperate countries such as France, Japan and Germany. The two main types of termite which attack timber in buildings are dry wood and subterranean termites. Of 1800 species, 10 per cent have been recorded as causing damage in buildings.

Termites are inconspicuous creatures living entirely inside the timber, often hollowing out large timbers, but leaving a thin shell for protection. Once begun, attack takes place largely within the timber and may well be advanced before being recognised. Termites have a well developed and complex colonial structure with each colony having winged adults, workers and soldiers.

Damage caused by other forms of animal and plant life

Higher forms of animal and plant life (Figure 8.6) also cause biodeterioration in buildings, for instance, rodents, birds and trees [10]. Next to human beings, rodents are the most successful mammal dwellers in buildings. Rodents are warm-blooded and therefore are adaptable to an extensive range of environmental conditions, from sub-zero cold stores to steamy tropical kitchens. The rat and mouse (family Muridae of the suborder Myomorphia) are mainly of concern as a pest

Figure 8.6 Plant damage to a building.

in buildings, for instance, *Rattus rattus* and *Mus musculus*. Rodents cause physical damage to building materials, owing to their constant gnawing, including damage to services such as pipework and electricity cables. They are also suspected of causing an unquantified but significant proportion of fires of 'unknown origin'. Their mere physical presence in the buildings is a nuisance with a particular regard to hygiene, disease transmission and health risk (see Section 8.4).

The problems caused by birds in buildings are the fouling of building exteriors with droppings, together with health (see Section 8.4) and hygiene risks due to nesting, roosting and dead birds. The most common bird pests in the UK are *Sturnus vulgaris* and feral pigeons *Columbia livia*.

Higher forms of plant life can colonise cracks and crevices in the stonework or brickwork of buildings. Plants exploit and help to create micro-environments suitable for microbial growth. Sometimes there is a succession of plants of increasing diversity and size. The surface of the stonework may first be colonised by micro-organisms and small algae, if conditions are suitable, followed by lichens and mosses which hold water, thus aiding physical weathering. Such plants help mineral and organic debris to accumulate and, eventually, a soil of sufficient depth and quality may be formed to allow the germination and growth of higher plants. The species of higher plants are diverse, ranging from small wood species through to woody shrubs and trees. The roots of woody perennials such as sycamore and yew may penetrate extensively through stones and brickwork and induce cracking of the structure.

Some higher plants are encouraged to grow near buildings, for example, creepers and vines, for aesthetic reasons. Such growth provides harbourage for other organisms such as birds and insects. The actual structure, for example, stone, brick or wood, may be penetrated by suckers or shoots causing physical damage.

Tree branches may grow outwards to touch buildings and, importantly, windows, thus causing damage as the tree grows further or sways in high winds. Other direct damage may be caused by tree roots, in that they can penetrate and block drains or water supply pipes and inflict considerable damage to the foundations of buildings. Indirect damage may be caused by roots absorbing water from the soil, leading to extensive soil shrinkage, especially in clay soils, where resorption of water may not restore the original conditions.

8.4 Biological health hazards

In England, 3.5 million homes are affected by condensation and damp [11]. Damp surfaces promote the growth of bacteria, moulds and mites. They are a risk to health and are associated with allergic illnesses. Published results indicate that 20 per cent of the population can be sensitised by air-borne fungal spores in the UK and 40 per cent of the inspected houses in Germany suffer from mould-related problems [12]. It is not appropriate to discuss here the medical consequences of immune response, allergic reactions, endotoxins, mycotoxins and epidemiology. The reader should consult the references and the further reading list at the end of the chapter for the relevant information (Morey *et al.* 1990). Similarly, legionnaires' disease and Pontiac fever are associated with wet cooling towers and domestic hot-water systems in complex buildings.

According to the official published figures, some 560 000 people need treatment because of indoor pollution due to mites and mould in damp houses [11]. Indoor air-borne allergic components come from two sources: outdoor air-borne spores moving inside and allergic components originating inside the dwelling. The source of biological growth within buildings is associated with moisture and the formation of micro-climates; it also depends upon the type of building and its ventilation. Mould fungi thrive on surfaces on which there is nourishment and suitable humidity, for example, damp water pipes, windows and walls in kitchens and bathrooms, central air-conditioning systems, central dehumidifiers and inside damp structures. Allergenic substances can be air borne and inhaled, such as pollen, fungus and dust, digested, such as mouldy food or drink, or be the result of physical contact, such as poison ivy. Investigations suggest that air-borne allergies cause more problems throughout the world than all other allergies combined. The medical field that treats allergies recognises the following allergenic diseases: asthma, allergic rhinitis, serous otitis media, bronchopulmonary aspergillosis and hypersensitivity pneumonitis.

Recently, attention has been focused on the cocktail effect of chemicals present in indoor air. Volatile organic compounds may be produced from the use of wood preservatives and remedial timber treatment chemicals, moth-proof carpets, fungicides, mouldicide-treated paints, furnishing materials such as particle board and foamed insulation which may emit formaldehyde [13]. Biological pollutants alone or in synergetic effect with any of the above-mentioned volatile organic compounds may produce symptoms such as a stuffy nose, dry throat, chest tightness, lethargy, loss of concentration, blocked, runny or itchy nose, dry skin, watering or itchy eyes and headache in sensitive people. The condition in which the occupants of a building experience these symptoms is called 'sick building syndrome' (SBS). Such symptoms may arise from a variety of causes. Because of the uncertainties about the causes of SBS and the rising levels of health-related problems in buildings there is an increasing use of the term building-related illness (BRI) to cover a range of ailments which commonly affect building occupants [11].

Fungal, viral, mycoplasmic and bacterial diseases in man and animals are world-wide in distribution. Many diseases in man and his pets are closely related and in a few cases some species can infect both, for example, fleas, mites, etc. In such cases, pets act as a reservoir of the inoculum and increase the chance that exposure to humans will lead to infection. Fungal infection of man and animals can be split into four categories: (1) Superficial, where the outer surface of the skin is invaded, for example, Tinea nigra disease of the palms and feet caused by *Cladosporium* spp. (2) Cutaneous, where the keratinised tissues of the body (outer epidermal cells of the skin, hair and nails) are invaded, for example, onychomycosis of the nails caused by *Aspergillus* sp and *Scopulariopsis* sp, and a number of diseases caused by *Candida* sp. (3) Subcutaneous, where invasion occurs in the deeper layers of the skin, for example, rhinosporidiosis affecting the nasal mucosa by *Rhinosporidium* sp and other skin diseases caused by *Aspergillus* sp. (4) Systemic, where infection of the lung takes place by direct inhalation of fungal spores. From the lungs the infection may be disseminated to all organs of the body and may cause death in man and his pets, for example, aspergillosis affecting the mucocutaneous tissue in the lung and skin caused by *Aspergillus fumigatus* and *Aspergillus* sp, and mucormycosis affecting the face, sinuses, gastrointestinal tract and lungs caused by *Mucor* sp and *Rhizopus* sp.

The cutaneous and subcutaneous mycoses are not considered air-borne diseases. Common air-borne systemic mycoses include: histoplasmosis caused by *Histoplasma capsulatum*, coccidioidomycosis caused by *Coccidioides immitis*, blastomycosis caused by *Blastomyces dermatitidis* and paracoccidioidomycosis caused by *Paracoccidiodides braziliensis*. Studies suggest that mycotoxins may play a role in the symptoms experienced by those building occupants who are heavily contaminated by certain fungal species. Mycotoxins are secondary metabolites produced by fungi. The most common mycotoxigenic fungi found in buildings are *Stachybotrys* sp, *Aspergillus* sp and *Penicillium* sp.

There are several species of fungi, bacteria and viruses which can cause contamination of food in houses. The most common species are *Bacillus* sp, *Lactobacillus* sp, *Clostridium* sp, *Botrytis* sp, *Penicillium* sp, *Aspergillus* sp. Among food-poisoning organisms the most common are *Salmonella* sp, *Staphylococcus* sp, *Clostridium* sp and *Bacillus* sp. At present there are 80 human pathogens among approximately 100 000 species of fungi.

In some building environments, insects, rodents and birds act as reservoirs of infection or vectors of diseases to man and his pets. An example of this is the association of bird roosting with the infection of school children by *Histoplasma capsulatum*. Pigeons are known to carry a mild form of psittacosis and *Salmonella*, which can be a potential health hazard. Rodents are known to transmit leptospirosis, trichinosis, rat bite fever, murine typhus fever, plague and salmonellosis.

8.5 Environmental assessment

Fungal growth is frequently observed in 10 per cent of the housing stock. The prerequisites for the development of mould fungi to contaminate indoor air are the presence of a nutrient medium, dampness and suitable temperature. Materials such as wallpaper, painted or plastic coated surfaces, insulating materials, textiles for interior work, floor coverings and wood and wood materials are potential food sources; non-nutrient materials such as plaster and brickwork can support growth by traces of contaminating organic matter. Mould fungi in general have a very wide temperature and humidity tolerance. However, relative humidities exceeding 70 per cent and temperatures in the range of 15–20°C are generally required [14].

There are several different techniques for the quantitative and qualitative enumeration of the biological agents in indoor air. The methods range from simple visual investigations and source sampling to complicated analytical methods of air sampling. There are environmental health centres in the UK, USA and elsewhere which have developed methods to enumerate the specific health-related problems associated with mould fungi in buildings [15]. Unfortunately, there are no government guidelines available for assessing numeric risk levels for airborne fungi. However, the BRE environmental assessment of new homes (BREEAM) covers the indoor issues. The emphasis is on the assessment of ventilation control systems, volatile organic pollutants, wood preservatives and non-gaseous indoor pollutants [16].

8.6 Environmental control

Biological health hazards and the biodeterioration of building materials is caused by a broad spectrum of fungi, bacteria, insects and other living organisms. In Sections 8.3 and 8.4, we have learnt about the nature of these destructive organisms. Remedial chemical treatment of these biological agents (both causing decay of material and affecting the health of the occupants) with fungicidal and insecticidal chemicals is often expensive, inconvenient, unnecessary, hazardous to operatives and occupants, and environmentally unacceptable [13]. Remedial treatment and extensive exposure work may be the result of panic, fear, despair and desperation induced by the reputation of these biological agents, particularly dry rot; it is frequently destructive. The eradication of biological agents from buildings is, in practice, impossible. The volumes of chemicals necessary and the toxicity required would be damaging both for the building and for its occupants. Environmental control and preventive maintenance are preferred to draconian chemical treatments, as they provide a long-term solution to the health of the building and its occupants [17–19].

Correct identification of the biological agent is important, as not all are equally destructive [6, 20]. For example, some rots may be present in timber when it is cut, or fungal or insect material may be dormant or dead, each of which represents conditions now past. By understanding the fundamental biology of the organism concerned, it is possible to discover the limits on the environmental conditions that allowed growth of the organism (Figure 8.7).

The environmental control policy for the biodeterioration of building materials should also encompass the following components: firstly, the non-destructive inspection of the building to locate and identify all the significant decay organisms within it, for example, the use of sniffer dogs and fibre-optic inspection techniques; and, secondly, to

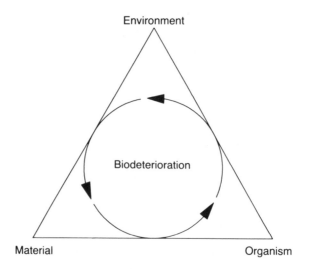

Figure 8.7   Biodeterioration cycle.

devise a scheme of remedial building techniques to deal with the problem, for example, the assessment of moisture content, relative humidity, microventilation and salt content. It is necessary to correct building defects, eliminate all sources of moisture, promote rapid drying and increase ventilation in vulnerable areas. Lastly, it is necessary to institute a programme of building maintenance and monitoring to prevent any future problems [17].

Environmental control of mould fungi in buildings must concentrate on reducing and eliminating the sources of water and water vapour. The desirable humidity of the air should range between 30 and 60 per cent, although a deviation of up to 10 per cent is justifiable if the quality of the air is good. Temperature should be maintained between 18 to 24°C depending upon the preference of the occupants. Regular cleaning and removal of the inoculum reservoirs and amplifiers helps to reduce the severity of the problem. Provision should be made for the installation of permanent extractor fans in bathroom and kitchen areas. All the closed cavities and voids, cupboards, roof spaces and floor spaces should be well ventilated.

8.7 Summary

- The growth and proliferation of biological agents and their effect on the health of the building fabric and its occupants in both modern and historic buildings can be attributed to changes in the building environment. A number of environmental, design and construction, shape and configuration, materials and structures, use and maintenance, and occupancy and management factors influence the building environment. These factors include building defects resulting in moisture associated with nutrient materials or detritus-enabling moulds, fungi, insects and higher organisms to take advantage of circumstances which favour their development. The main environmental factors favouring the growth of biological agents in buildings are water, humidity, temperature and lack of ventilation.

- Building biology affects the health of building occupants. The influencing factors are microbiological growth including fungi, moulds, viruses, insects, bacteria, mites, pollen, algae and other allergens. People complain about fatigue, headaches, skin irritation, mucus membrane trouble and smell. The medical field recognises the following allergenic diseases: asthma, allergic rhinitis, serous otitis media, bronchopulmonary aspergillosis and hypersensitivity pneumonitis. The effects of building biology on the health of building structures, contents and decorations are well documented. Among the influencing factors are the biodeterioration of timber caused by fungi (dry rot and wet rot fungi) and insects (deathwatch beetle and woodworm).

- The concept of the eradication of biological agents from within buildings is practically impossible. The remedial approach often involves considerable reliance on the use of chemicals and extensive exposure of the building fabric. This has a detrimental effect on the health of the building fabric, its occupants and is environmentally damaging. Potential environmental and occupational disadvantages of remedial chemical treatments together with doubts over its long-term effectiveness lead to the development and reliance on the concepts of environmental control strategies.

- Environmental control relies on an understanding of construction details and the biology of the organism concerned, including its environmental requirements. This is followed by alteration or removal of the favourable environment for the life cycle of the organism. By manipulating the environment of the organism, the growth of biological agents can be arrested. Monitoring the building environment, including the installation of remote sensing systems, can give advance warnings of the failure of the building fabric [21].

References

1. B. Walker, *Allergic Reactions in Buildings* (Building Services, 1991).
2. M. Schimmelschmidt, 'Breathing life into housing', *RIBA Journal* (1990), pp. 56–9.
3. W. Bordass, 'The effects – for good and ill – of building services and their controls', in T. Bahns *et al.* (ed.), *Proceedings of the Building Pathology Conference* organised by Singh and Hutton (Guildford: Hutton & Rostron, 1989), pp. 6–9 and 39–69.
4. J. Singh, *Biological Control of Late Blight Fungus*, Phd thesis for University of London, 1986.
5. J. Singh, 'Investigation and advice on refurbishment of building after fire damage', *Construction Repair*, **3**(7) (1989), pp. 26–30.
6. J. Singh, 'Ecology and environmental control of timber decay in buildings', *Construction Repair*, **3**(3) (1989), pp. 26–30.
7. J. Singh, 'Timber decay, don't panic and poison yourself', *Kent Seen* (1989), pp. 32–4.
8. J. Singh, 'Biodeterioration of building materials', in K. Garg *et al.* (ed.), *Recent Advances in Biodeterioration* (Florida: CRC, In press).
9. B. King *et al.*, *A Summary of Current Information on Actinomycetes and Wood* (The international research group on wood preservation, Document no IRG/WP/177, 1978).
10. D. Allsopp and K. L. Seal, *Introduction to Biodeterioration* (London: Edward Arnold, 1986), p. 135.
11. House of Commons, Environment Committee Sixth report, *Indoor Pollution*, Vol. 1 (London: HMSO, 1991).
12. N. V. Waubke and W. Kusterle, *Mould Infestation in Residential Buildings* (Innsbruck, 1990).
13. *Toxic Treatments*, A London Hazards Centre handbook (1988).
14. Building Research Establishment, *Mould Growth in Buildings* (Watford: BRE, 1981).
15. J. Munro, Allergy and Environmental Medicine Ltd, Breakspear Hospital, Hertfordshire, UK.
16. BRE BREEAM, New homes version 3/91, *An Environmental Assessment for New Homes* (Watford: BRE, 1991).
17. T. C. Hutton, H. R. Lloyd and J. Singh, 'The environmental control of timber decay', *Structural Survey*, **10**(1) (1991), pp. 5–21.
18. J. Singh 'Environmental control of timber decay', in T. Bahns *et al.* (ed.), *Proceedings of the Building Pathology Conference* organised by Singh and Hutton (Guildford: Hutton & Rostron, 1989), pp. 108–21.
19. J. Singh and J. Faull, 'Antagonism and biological control', in K. G.

of practice might be the limits of the requirements of a notice; at least the local authority must have regard to their provisions.

Noise level is an area where the EC has become involved following a whole range of council directives relating to the permissible sound level of construction plant and equipment. Formal compliance with the directives was achieved by the Construction Plant and Equipment (Harmonisation of Noise Emission Standards) Regulations 1985. These provide for two sets of limits: the first came into force in March 1986, while the second, more stringent, standards became effective in September 1989. Compliance with the noise limits is to be assured by a certification procedure, run for the government by consultancies accredited under the National Testing Accreditation Scheme.

Pollution of the water environment

Any serious pollution of the water environment during building operations is likely to give rise to prosecution by the NRA under the Water Resources Act 1991. The Act sets out the statutory system for the control by the NRA of pollution of inland and coastal waters, including lakes and ponds, and the increasingly important problem of groundwater pollution (the Act refers to all these waters as controlled waters). It is an offence under Section 85 to cause or knowingly permit any poisonous, noxious or polluting matter or any solid waste matter to enter any controlled waters. It is not necessary to show that a defendant acted intentionally or negligently to be found guilty of an offence. It is a defence to show that any discharge into controlled waters was in accordance with a consent or disposal licence issued by the NRA, or in certain circumstances, if a discharge is made in an emergency, in order to avoid danger to life or health. Conviction will bring a current maximum fine of £20 000 in the Magistrates' Court and/or a term of imprisonment not exceeding three months, or an unlimited fine and/or imprisonment not exceeding two years, if proceedings are brought in the Crown Court for more serious offences. The Act also gives wide-ranging powers to the NRA to carry out work to protect or restore the environment, including the flora and fauna, at the expense of those who cause pollution.

The offences under the Water Resources Act are capable of covering water-borne pollution generated during the course of construction works and discharged into a water course, or into the ground subsequently leading to pollution of groundwater. The occupier of any trade premises within the area of a sewerage undertaker (the recently privatised regional water and sewerage authorities – water companies) may with the consent of the undertaker discharge any trade effluent from the premises into the public sewers. Trade premises means any premises used or intended to be used for carrying on trade or industry. Application has to be made by written notice to a sewerage undertaker for a consent to discharge trade effluent from any trade premises into the public sewer. The sewerage undertaker may give consent either unconditionally or subject to such conditions as it thinks fit, including specifying the sewer to which discharge is to be made, the nature or composition of the trade effluent, the maximum volume which may be discharged and the period during which trade effluent may be discharged. If trade effluent is discharged without a consent or in contravention of a condition, the occupier of the premises is guilty of an offence and liable on conviction in the Magistrates' Court to a fine in 1992 not exceeding £20 000, and on conviction in the Crown Court to an unlimited fine for more serious offences.

Proposed discharges of effluent containing the so-called 'red list' substances, for example, mercury, cadmium, PCBs, have to be referred by the sewerage undertakers to the Secretary of State for the Environment for his consent. Given their danger to the aquatic environment, they are subject to even more stringent control.

Waste on land

Under the EPA, from 1 April 1992, it became necessary for contractors to comply with an innovative duty of care in respect of controlled waste generated by construction operations. Controlled waste includes household, industrial and commercial waste. The duty is to take all measures reasonable in the circumstances to the following ends:

- to prevent any contravention by any person of the prohibition on the unauthorised deposit, treatment or disposal of controlled waste;
- to prevent the escape of controlled waste from his or any other person's control;
- on the transfer of controlled waste, to secure that the transfer is only to an authorised person or for authorised transport purposes; and, in either case, to ensure that the waste is accompanied by an adequate written description (a transfer note).

Authorised persons include waste collection authorities, those holding waste disposal or waste management licences, and registered carriers. As from 14 October 1991, all building, construction and demolition contractors were required to register their companies or themselves under the Controlled Waste (Registration of Carriers and Seizure of Vehicles) Regulations 1991 and are themselves subject to the duty of care as from 1 April 1992. These regulations implement the Control of Pollution (Amendment) Act 1989 and make it an offence for any person to transport controlled waste in the course of his business, or in any way for profit, without being registered. The carrier may be stopped and required to produce his authority for transporting controlled waste. There is no provision in the Act or the regulations that they should apply only to transport on the public highway. Thus moving waste materials from one side of a construction site to the other necessitates owner registration.

It will be necessary to keep records of waste produced and how it was disposed of off site. Failure to comply with the duty or to keep appropriate records may result in a fine of currently up to £2000 in the Magistrates' Court, or an unlimited fine in the Crown Court in the case of more serious offences. This will depend in part on whether the code of practice issued by the Secretary of State for the Environment has been followed.

A circular, regulations, and a code of practice have been issued by the DoE to help business and regulators to implement this duty of care. The regulations define the documentation required to be kept by all parties involved in a transfer of controlled waste (including transfer notes), the steps that will be considered reasonable and the length of time for retaining records (at least two years). The intention is to ensure that 'cradle to grave' control is implemented, with the duty of care resulting in each person in the chain having an interest in ensuring that the next person obeys the law. Advisable practice in future will be for any person disposing of waste off site to find a registered carrier, check with the local authority that the carrier is in fact registered, prepare a description of the waste transferred and exchange this for a receipt (together these will form the transfer note). In many cases it will be typical to incorporate transfer notes into existing invoices.

Air pollution and statutory nuisances

Part I of the EPA establishes systems for the granting of authorisations by the HMIP for what are likely to be about 5000 of the most seriously polluting industrial plant. The system is known as 'integrated pollution control' and covers emissions to air, land and water. Part I also establishes a system of air pollution control, to be administered by the local authorities, which is likely to cover some 25 to 30 000 plants causing air pollution. Integrated pollution control and air pollution control require plant operators to obtain an authorisation for their particular process, which will contain anti-pollution conditions. Although building operations are not prescribed processes requiring authorisation under Part I, a building contractor could be prosecuted under Part III of the EPA, which is concerned with statutory nuisances and clean air, and is primarily focused on threats to public health or hygiene. However, where there are such threats, action can also be taken to protect the environment.

Should building operations give rise to smoke, dust, steam, smell, or other effluvia, or to any accumulation or deposit which amounts to a nuisance, or any noise emitted from premises, the local authority can seek to abate the nuisance by serving an abatement notice on the person responsible. Nuisance is not defined in the EPA and should be understood in its common law sense.

The local authority has a duty to inspect its area from time to time in order to detect possible statutory nuisances which ought to be abated. An abatement notice may require the abatement or restriction of an existing nuisance, or the prohibition or restriction of a nuisance which may occur in the future; or the taking of such other steps or the execution of such works as may be necessary to achieve this. Failure to comply with the notice without reasonable cause within the time limit specified in the notice is an offence liable on conviction in the Magistrates' Court to a fine of currently up to £20 000, with an additional fine of 10 per cent of this amount payable on a daily basis until the nuisance is abated. If there is a default in compliance, a local authority may now take action to remedy the nuisance without first going to court. Where an abatement notice has not been complied with, the local authority may take the necessary steps to abate the nuisance itself consistent with the terms of the abatement notice and recover any costs reasonably incurred from the person responsible for the nuisance.

A defence to the statutory nuisance proceedings mentioned above is available where 'best practicable means' were used to prevent or counteract the effects of the nuisance. The EPA states that 'practicable' should be interpreted as meaning reasonably practicable, having regard among other things to local conditions and circumstances, to the current state of technical knowledge and to the financial implications. The 'means' to be employed include the design, installation, maintenance and manner and periods of occupation of plant and machinery, and the design, construction and maintenance of buildings and structures.

A major new development is the provision of a procedure by which private individuals aggrieved by a statutory nuisance can seek relief in the Magistrates' Court. The procedure only applies where a nuisance exists or has existed, and so no anticipatory relief is afforded. If the magistrates are satisfied that the alleged nuisance exists or is likely to recur, they will make an order requiring the abatement of the nuisance within a stated time limit, the execution of any necessary remedial works, and/or prohibiting the recurrence of the nuisance and requiring any works to be carried out to prevent such recurrence within a specified period. The proceedings can be brought either against the person responsible for the nuisance or, if that person cannot be found, against the owner or occupier of the premises on which the nuisance has arisen.

Failure to comply with an abatement notice, where there is no reasonable excuse, is also made an offence. This is punishable by a fine, which increases for every day on which the offence continues after the conviction. In certain circumstances the defence that the best practicable means were used to prevent or counteract the effects of the nuisance is available.

In addition, it should be remembered that where building operations cause environmental damage to adjoining or neighbouring properties, there are a whole range of common law remedies that could be available to adjoining owners who have suffered loss or damage, including actions for trespass to land and private nuisance, the latter being the unlawful interference with a person's use and enjoyment of land or some right over or in connection with it. Negligence actions could also be brought, though in the case of negligence an interest in adjoining or neighbouring land is not a prerequisite.

Liability might also arise under the principle established in Rylands versus Fletcher [2], where it was held that the person who brings on to his land and collects and keeps there anything likely to do mischief if it escapes, must keep it at his peril and, if he does not do so, is prima facie answerable for all the damage which is the natural consequence of its escape. Although this gives rise to strict (no fault) liability, the usefulness of this principle has been weakened by the courts' unwillingness to give an extended meaning to 'non-natural' user of land, which has to be established if an action is to be successfully maintained. For example, in a recent case [3] the High Court ruled that a water company had no remedy under Rylands versus Fletcher against a tannery for historical pollution of groundwater caused by a solvent seeping into the groundwater and causing a borehole and associated water-supply works being taken out of use.

Interaction with health and safety legislation

The Health and Safety at Work, etc, Act 1974 is principally concerned with worker protection, not protection of the environment. Nevertheless, it is intended that there will be full cooperation between the

Health and Safety Executive and their agents on the one hand and the HMIP and local authority inspectors on the other to ensure that the controls they are respectively responsible for are effective and compatible. It is the DoE's intention that where environmental protection demands tighter standards of control than are required to safeguard persons at work, these tighter standards should apply, provided they have no adverse effects on worker protection.

The Health and Safety at Work, etc, Act 1974 and its numerous associated regulations govern many aspects of building occupation, such as legionnaires' disease, indoor air quality and ventilation. In addition, the use of most common chemicals found in buildings is also subject to the health and safety regulations, in particular the Control of Substances Hazardous to Health Regulations 1988.

9.5 Occupied buildings

A completed commercial building can be put to many different uses, subject of course to limitations imposed by the Town and Country Planning Acts, fire regulations and any covenants restricting use imposed by a landlord or an adjoining owner. Pollution of any environmental media, whether it be land, water or the air, originating from the building can therefore give rise to liability; in this respect the earlier sections of this chapter are applicable. For example, atmospheric emissions could lead to statutory nuisance proceedings being brought by the local authority, or a neighbouring owner bringing proceedings for private nuisance. Discharges of polluting substances into water courses could bring prosecution by the NRA or, indeed, a private prosecution by a concerned individual or a pressure group. Discharge of effluent into sewers without the appropriate consent will enable the sewerage undertaker to bring proceedings in the Magistrates' Court under the Water Industry Act 1991. Any permanent deposits of controlled waste on land, in the absence of the requisite waste disposal or a waste management licence, will also give rise to liability. The penalties for these offences enable magistrates to impose a prison sentence of up to six months and/or a fine of currently up to £20 000. In the Crown Court, the penalties are increased to two years and/or an unlimited fine for more serious offences. Where more hazardous, special waste [4] is involved, the maximum prison sentence increases to five years.

9.6 Demolition

Demolition of commercial buildings can give rise to many of the same problems occurring at the construction stage. Noise, dust, polluted water and waste materials can all arise. What has been said earlier is therefore relevant. Particular regard will have to be paid to the proper disposal of waste, because of the new statutory duty of care covering the disposal of controlled waste and registration requirements affecting demolition contractors.

9.7 Future developments

In July 1991, the government indicated that it proposed establishing an environmental protection agency which would draw together all or part of the NRA, HMIP, the waste regulatory functions of the local authorities and the Drinking Water Inspectorate. Discussion has tended to centre on how this would affect the NRA: would it be transferred entirely to this new agency, or would just the anti-pollution role be transferred, leaving other functions, such as land drainage, to be taken over by the Ministry of Agriculture? After an extensive public consultation, the government announced in July 1992 that the new agency would bring together the NRA, HMIP and waste regulation from local government.

With the approach of the single market, the EC is taking an ever-more prominent role in initiating new environmental legislation. By 1992 there were over 300 items of EC legislation in the environmental field. The framework for the EC's environmental policy is contained in its action programmes, which are similar to government white papers. These are drawn up by the EC and then go to the Council of Ministers for approval. A fifth action programme has been drafted by the EC, covering the period 1993 to 2000. This was likely to build on recent developments, including improving implementation by member states, integrating environmental concerns into other areas of policy and the use of economic instruments, for example, energy taxes and tradeable permits.

Areas where further EC action is likely are:

- Civil liability for damage caused by waste. A proposed directive would introduce a system of strict liability on producers of waste unless and until the waste was transferred to an authorised disposal facility. Recent indications suggest that this directive will not proceed; instead, there will be a directive dealing with civil liability for all activities which damage the environment, not just waste.

- Environmental assessment of policies, plans and programmes: a draft directive was being prepared in 1992 by the EC to extend the principles of environmental assessment from projects to policies, plans and programmes, for example, structure and local plans.
- European Environment Agency: this Agency was agreed on in 1990, but its development was held up by a political argument over its location. The Agency is intended to provide the EC and member states with objective, reliable and comparable environmental information at community level. It will coordinate information from a network of national organisations. It could of course form the basis for a community-wide environmental enforcement agency.

9.8 Summary

- Government policy is to frame laws that will prevent, rather than cure, pollution.
- The polluter is to pay for the pollution generated.
- Environmental protection laws will be increasingly initiated by the EC unless the controversial subsidiarity principle, referred to in the Treaty of Maastricht, is applied.
- Environmental protection will become an ever-more significant factor in town and country planning.
- New contaminated land registers under the EPA could have a significant impact on the location of commercial developments and on the availability of development finance, if the government proceeds with its proposals.
- Building regulations whilst not primarily concerned with environmental protection will give greater consideration to issues such as energy efficiency and the use of environmentally friendly building materials.
- Construction operations must be carried out in such a manner so as to cause no unavoidable pollution of the air, land or water.
- Waste materials must be disposed of in accordance with the new duty of care imposed by the EPA, and only by registered contractors.
- The government plans a new, comprehensive Environment Agency for England and Wales, but this is unlikely to be in place until 1994.

References

1. Department of Environment Consultation Paper, July 1992.
2. *Rylands* versus *Fletcher* (1868) LR3 HL 330.

☆	Poor
☆☆	Standard
☆☆☆	Good
☆☆☆☆	Very good
☆☆☆☆☆	Excellent

As well as giving a star rating, the certificate estimates annual carbon dioxide emissions arising from this level of energy efficiency. Furthermore, information is given on projects which would confer a higher star rating, together with the cost of implementing this work, estimated reductions in annual fuel bills and estimated reductions in annual carbon dioxide emission. Assessment can be arranged through Starpoint in Bristol.

10.6 Product labelling

The European Commission has an environmental labelling scheme (or 'ecolabel') for products, which will be administered in Britain by the UK Ecolabelling Board from 1 November 1992. The aim is that the first 'ecolabelled' products will be available in 1993, but construction materials are likely to take longer than this. It is hoped that this information will stimulate demand for products with a lower environmental impact and, in this way, encourage the development and launch of new products.

It is intended that the label will indicate not only environmental performance in use, but also at the production and disposal stages. Thus, the impact from the cradle to the grave will be included. Whilst it will take some time for a wide range of products to be assessed, when the regulations are implemented in each of the member states they will provide a useful additional decision-making tool for all of those concerned with the environmental performance of buildings. Product labelling will never take the place of an environmental assessment of a complete building, because only this wider assessment will consider all of the necessary issues.

10.7 Summary

- A structured approach is necessary to appraise successfully the environmental impact of any building.
- There are a variety of ways to assess environmental performance from the creation of an environmental policy based upon the information in this book to the use of a proprietary assessment method.

- Building Research Establishment environmental assessment method (BREEAM) version 1/90 assesses the performance of new office schemes.
- BREEAM 2/91 assesses the environmental impact of new supermarkets and superstores.
- BREEAM 3/91 advises on the performance of new homes.
- Watts & Partners' environmental survey gives practical advice tailored to the requirements of specific clients and individual buildings.
- Environmental impact assessments are sometimes necessary when making a planning application.
- The National Home Energy Rating Scheme and the Starpoint Home Energy Labels are two British methods for assessing energy efficiency of homes. The bodies responsible for these schemes are now implementing the government's standard assessment procedure.
- The European Commission has a scheme for environmental labelling of products, including some building materials. Products with 'ecolabels' are expected to appear from 1993.

References

1. R. Lorch, *What Are You Doing About the Environment? The Specifier and Building Materials* (London: Junior Liaison Organisation, 1989), p. 2.
2. Town and Country Planning (Assessment of Environmental Effects) Regulations 1988.

Further reading

R. Baldwin, S. Leach, J. Doggart and M. Attenborough, *BREEAM 1/90 – An Environmental Assessment for New Office Designs* (Watford: BRE, 1990).

British Standards Institution, *BS 7750: 1992 – British Standard Specification for Environmental Management Systems* (London: BSI, 1992).

V. Crisp, J. Doggart and M. Attenborough, *BREEAM 2/91 – An Environmental Assessment for New Superstores and Supermarkets* (Watford: BRE, 1991).

M. Day and M. Davis, 'Environmental assessment regulations – response of the development sector', *Estates Gazette*, **9028** (14 July 1990), pp. 48–50.

'Mainly for students – environmental assessment', *Estates Gazette*, **8931** (5 August 1989), pp. 63–4.

F. Ghigny, 'Energy certification of buildings – proposal for a directive of the Commission of the European Communities', in EURIMA, European Insulation Manufacturers' Association, *Energy Audits in Buildings* – Text of the presentations at a meeting organised by the EC DG XVII/EURIMA in Brussels on 13 May 1991 (Brussels: Eurima, 1991).

MVM Starpoint Limited, Clifton Heights, Triangle West, Bristol BS8 1EJ, tel: 0272 253769.

National Home Energy Rating Scheme, The National Energy Foundation, Rockingham Drive, Linford Wood, Milton Keynes MK14 6EG, tel: 0908 672787.

J. Prior, G. Raw and J. Charlesworth, *BREEAM/New Homes Version 3/91 – An Environmental Assessment for New Homes* (Watford: BRE, 1991).

J. Smit, 'Green machine', *New Builder* (21 February 1991), pp. 22–3.

Watts & Partners' environmental survey, Watts & Partners, 11–12 Haymarket, London SW1Y 4BP, tel: 071-930 6652.

11 Conclusions
Stuart Johnson

11.1 Introduction

The introductory chapter to this book states that a building's environmental impact extends from global factors such as ozone depletion to the quality of the environment inside the property. These impacts arise from decisions made at all stages of a building's life, including materials manufacture, site selection, design, construction, occupation and ultimately demolition. As environmental impact arises from all stages of a building's life, a contribution is made by all parties involved in property, including materials manufacturers, contractors, architects, surveyors and other professionals, financiers, funding institutions, developers, occupiers, students and so on. For these reasons a building's environmental impact arises from the complex interrelationships between many different topics, from the type of building materials which have been used to the orientation of the building and the way in which it is occupied.

Rather than build an understanding of these interrelationships some prefer to adopt standard solutions for dealing with individual environmental issues. For example, upon reading this book, it could be thought that buildings should always have high levels of thermal insulation to enhance the occupiers' comfort and minimise energy consumption. Unfortunately, standard solutions such as this are not always appropriate as there are unlikely to be good reasons for insulating a building which is not to be provided with space heating. On environmental grounds, the reason for this is that it is conceivable that more energy will be consumed in the production and installation of thermal insulation than would ever be saved by reducing heat loss during the building's life. It is all too easy to lose sight of circumstances like this when implementing standard solutions.

Some people advocate going even further and adopting a blacklist of materials and items of plant which should be prohibited from buildings on environmental grounds. An example could be that wet cooling towers shall not be used because of the risk of legionnaires' disease. However, it is important to remember that environmental impact arises not only from the selection of specific materials and items of plant, but also from the way in which they are used. Returning to our example, wet cooling towers can be used successfully where an appropriate maintenance and testing regime is in place. To prohibit the use of such items of equipment may well be to deny the most appropriate design solution.

As the environmental performance of buildings cannot be enhanced meaningfully whilst considering single issues in isolation, this chapter has been set out in the same way as the whole book, namely, first, individual environmental issues are dealt with and, later, these individual threads are drawn together by overall conclusions which stress the need for a coordinated approach. Whilst the priority given to each issue will inevitably vary according to individual circumstances, it may be helpful to bear in mind that ozone depletion and carbon dioxide emissions are generally considered the most significant concerns at present. Thus, measures to lessen their impact should be given special attention.

11.2 Environmental issues

- Our use of chlorofluorocarbons (CFCs) is depleting the ozone layer and thus reducing its efficiency at screening the earth from harmful ultraviolet light.
- CFCs should not be used, but where this is not possible or appropriate, compounds which result in the least harm to the ozone layer should be preferred and measures taken to avoid release to the atmosphere.
- Increased emissions of carbon dioxide, CFCs, methane and other greenhouse gases are resulting in global warming.
- A significant proportion of greenhouse gases arise from electricity generation and we should strive to improve the energy efficiency of our buildings to mitigate global warming.
- Sulphur dioxide is the main cause of acid rain. In the UK, over 70 per cent of sulphur dioxide is attributable to power stations. This is another reason for increasing energy efficiency of buildings on environmental grounds.
- The bacteria Legionella has an adverse effect on the neighbourhood environment and care must be taken not to create conditions for its release into the atmosphere.
- Building services directly influence the quality of the internal environment. Care must be taken with the original installation and subsequent maintenance that the conditions created fall within

normally accepted temperature and humidity limits. Failure to do so can result in a case of sick building syndrome.

- Our choice of building materials affects the internal environment. We should be aware of the health implications of the products which we specify both to the applicators and building users.
- Insects, pests and micro-organisms can affect the health of building occupants. Construction and maintenance should strive to reduce their effect to a minimum.

11.3 Site hazards

- Development sites may be contaminated by former industrial uses. Thorough site investigation is essential to avoid unnecessary risks to health and safety or costly unplanned remedial work. The aim is to identify hazardous substances present, their distribution, and their concentrations at and below the surface.
- A preliminary investigation should include a thorough review of site history, geology, hydrology and neighbouring land use. This review and a site reconnaissance are used to devise a detailed sampling plan.
- The main purpose of a full environmental site investigation is to assess environmental hazards and risks, and to judge whether remedial action is necessary for the proposed end use. There are many specialist technologies for remediation of contaminated soil and groundwater but, for some, little expertise and experience is available in the UK.
- Landfill gas is an additional problem on some sites and can give rise to fire, explosion and asphyxiation risks. It can migrate for considerable distances and may persist as a problem for decades after a landfill is completed. Special protective measures and rigorous long-term monitoring may be called for when developing on or near landfill sites.
- Radon, an inert gas derived from the radioactive decay of uranium, can build up in poorly ventilated indoor spaces. When inhaled over long periods the daughter products of radon cause radiation damage to the lungs which can result in cancer.
- In the UK, indoor radon concentrations are highest in Cornwall where an active programme has identified areas and properties most at risk. Radon sumps, from which the gas can be safely vented to the atmosphere, have proved effective in reducing indoor radon concentrations. A membrane barrier can reduce radon ingress if carefully fitted but the most effective methods are underfloor ventilation and suction.

- Overhead power lines generate very low-frequency electromagnetic fields which have been implicated in a range of adverse health effects. However, the evidence is far from clear and the issue is controversial. The evidence for a small excess risk of cancer (especially leukaemia) in children may be insufficient but, pending further research, it may still be prudent to avoid developments within 100 metres of high-voltage transmission lines that would result in long exposure times for children.

11.4 Architecture and landscape

- Ensure that the design of a new building is developed by the architect working in close consultation with all of the other design disciplines from the conceptual stages through detailed design and construction.
- Consider the siting of a new building with particular attention to the natural characteristics of the site to make every effort to build on reasonably flat, dry land and avoiding steeply sloping sites, flood plains and high quality agricultural land.
- Orientate new buildings to create outdoor and indoor spaces which will benefit from sun, views and shelter from the wind.
- Design clearly articulated systems of structure and environmental servicing and ensure that they are carefully coordinated and integrated together.
- Consider the palette of materials from which a building will be constructed for its appropriateness with regard to surroundings, performance and long life.
- Examine the design of the external skin of the building with reference to both its aesthetic qualities and its function. Ensure that it is highly insulated and that glazed areas are designed to provide good levels of daylighting internally but avoid excessive solar gain and glare.
- Investigate the opportunities to specify materials which have low primary energy consumption yet have a long life.
- Test and evaluate the environmental systems of new buildings in design and monitor them wherever possible once in use.

11.5 Energy efficiency

- Energy consumed through our use of buildings is a significant contributor to environmental costs such as global warming and acid rain. There is increasing pressure to enhance energy efficiency to reduce pollution.

- Many energy efficiency measures are cost effective.
- There is an argument that inefficient buildings will become less desirable and therefore less valuable.
- Regulations and legislation affecting energy performance are becoming more stringent and it does not take a great stretch of the imagination to anticipate that more efficient energy use may become mandatory.
- There are many components to the energy efficiency of buildings, from the insulation standard of building fabric to the performance of services plant. All of these aspects must be considered during design and construction, occupation and maintenance.
- The starting point for determining the level of insulation for new buildings is the building regulations. The Approved Document suggests a number of ways for meeting the required level of performance.
- Levels of thermal insulation required for new buildings have increased and this process is likely to continue, especially with forthcoming legislation from the European Commission.
- There is a strong argument for using greater levels of thermal insulation in new buildings than the Building Regulations 1991 demand. However, the level adopted will depend upon a number of factors and each building should be considered separately.
- High levels of thermal insulation may result in non-traditional construction and materials. Care should be taken to minimise the risk of failure.
- Materials from local sources should be chosen wherever possible in order to minimise the energy consumed during the journey to site.
- The processing and manufacture of building materials uses energy. Little information is available, but in general terms the greater the amount of processing the more energy is used. This should be borne in mind when choices are made.
- At the design stage, care should be taken to maximise durability and flexibility in order to avoid premature failure or obsolescence.
- Out-of-town schemes usually imply a high degree of fuel use in transporting building users from their homes; therefore, the whole scheme may be very inefficient in energy terms.
- The way in which we have viewed the investment potential of buildings has maintained the proliferation of energy-dependent internal environments and stifled the introduction of more natural methods of moderating occupied spaces.
- HVAC and other artificial environmental moderators are very high energy users. The 'bolt on' energy-saving measures that are available may well be contributing to the overall reduction in energy

usage, but to make real strides, radical approaches are required. The eradication of artificial environmental conditioning by using the building itself as the environmental moderator is the way forward.

- A holistic approach to building creation can easily make inroads into the very heart of energy use and can provide the platform for encouraging buildings in equilibrium.

- There is a trade-off between initial and running costs, or the costs of energy-saving measures against fuel bills. Life cycle costing is a procedure for identifying the present value of total costs throughout the life of the building which allows effective decision making between different options.

11.6 Building materials

- There is an environmental dimension to our use of all building materials. The products dealt with in Chapter 6 are some of the main ones, but many principles used apply elsewhere, too.

- The use of tropical hardwoods from non-sustainable sources has a number of environmental consequences. Wherever possible, care should be taken to ensure that tropical hardwoods come from sustainable sources. Where this is not possible, alternative materials can be selected.

- Chlorofluorocarbons contribute to the depletion of the ozone layer and also add to the greenhouse effect. CFCs and associated compounds are found in some insulating materials, fire-extinguishing systems, air-conditioning plant and refrigeration equipment. Their use should be avoided wherever possible, but where they are considered necessary, compounds with the lowest possible ozone-depleting factor should be selected and measures taken to avoid release to the atmosphere.

- As a result of the health risks, asbestos is not generally specified for new work. Where asbestos is discovered in existing buildings, a structured approach should be followed, and where encapsulation or removal is appropriate, only suitably licensed contractors should be used.

- There are health implications in the use of solvent-based paints. Water-based paints are being developed and becoming more widely available. Subject to appropriate performance these new products should be used when unacceptable levels of vapour may occur if solvent-based paints are applied.

- Alternatives are available for most uses of toxic lead-based paints and these should be selected.

- Many timber treatments are toxic and therefore their use should be minimised and carefully controlled. An alternative is to obviate the need for timber treatments by careful design and detailing.
- Formaldehyde vapour arising from the use of urea formaldehyde foam insulation in cavity walls can cause a number of harmful symptoms in building occupants. Its use is restricted in new work and remedial action may be necessary where it is found in existing buildings.
- Formaldehyde is also found in some processed timber boards. The cautious approach is to use low-emission boards.
- Recycled or second-hand building components should be considered wherever possible to reduce the environmental impact of building operations.
- Buildings should be soundly detailed using durable materials and be as flexible as possible in order to maximise their useful life. Such an approach implies that the environmental impact of buildings will be minimised because good use will be made of finite materials.
- Our knowledge of the environmental impact of building materials is changing rapidly and there is a need to keep abreast with new products and research.

11.7 Engineering services

- The Industrial Revolution dramatically changed the manner in which buildings affected the human body. We have solved most of the fatal effects but we have yet to properly address and solve the effects that reduce performance or impair well-being.
- Employee costs are now so significant that inefficiencies have a major impact upon the profitability and competitiveness of organisations.
- Internal environmental conditioning can be naturally or artificially created. The demands upon modern buildings from users and office equipment require substantial environmental and building services systems. The systems dramatically affect the form and shape of structures.
- If a building can be designed with the impact of external influences as well as internal influences being controlled, the environmental systems can be minimised.
- In addition to air quality and quantity issues, the ability of building users to relate to outside conditions and to control their own personal environments has a marked effect upon well-being and satisfaction.

- The selection of heating, ventilation and air-conditioning (HVAC) systems is a major contributory factor when attempting to create thermal comfort and to minimise the way in which buildings impact on the human body.
- The future success of any modern building will therefore depend upon a whole range of influencing factors that are the domain of the environmental and building services engineer. A new breed of such engineers are creating solutions to match the future expectations – that of responsible buildings.

11.8 Building biology and health

- The growth and proliferation of biological agents and their effect on the health of the building fabric and its occupants in both modern and historic buildings can be attributed to changes in the building environment. A number of environmental, design and construction, shape and configuration, materials and structures, use and maintenance and occupancy and management factors influence the building environment. These factors include building defects resulting in moisture associated with nutrient materials or detritus-enabling moulds, fungi, insects and higher organisms to take advantage of circumstances which favour their development. The main environmental factors favouring the growth of biological agents in buildings are water, humidity, temperature and lack of ventilation.
- Building biology affects the health of building occupants. The influencing factors are microbiological growth, including fungi, moulds, viruses, insects, bacteria, mites, pollen, algae and other allergens. People complain about fatigue, headaches, skin irritation, mucus membrane trouble and smell. The medical field recognises the following allergenic diseases: asthma, allergic rhinitis, serous otitis media, bronchopulmonary aspergillosis and hypersensitivity pneumonitis. The effects of building biology on the health of building structures, contents and decorations are well documented. Among the influencing factors are the biodeterioration of timber caused by fungi (dry rot and wet rot fungi) and insects (deathwatch beetle and woodworm).
- The concept of the eradication of biological agents from within buildings is practically impossible. The remedial approach often involves considerable reliance on the use of chemicals and extensive exposure of the building fabric. This has a detrimental effect on the health of the building fabric and its occupants, and is environmentally damaging. Potential environmental and

occupational disadvantages of remedial chemical treatments together with doubts over its long-term effectiveness lead to the development and reliance on the concepts of environmental control strategies.

- Environmental control relies on an understanding of construction details and the biology of the organism concerned, including its environmental requirements. This is followed by alteration or removal of the favourable environment for the life cycle of the organism. By manipulating the environment of the organism, the growth of biological agents can be arrested. Monitoring the building environment, including the installation of remote sensing systems, can give advance warnings of the failure of the building fabric.

11.9 Environmental law

- Government policy is to frame laws that will prevent, rather than cure, pollution.
- The polluter is to pay for the pollution generated.
- Environmental protection laws will be increasingly initiated by the EC unless the controversial subsidiarity principle, referred to in the Treaty of Maastricht, is applied.
- Environmental protection will become an ever-more significant factor in town and country planning.
- New contaminated land registers under the EPA could have a significant impact on the location of commercial developments and on the availability of development finance, if the government proceeds with its proposals.
- Building regulations whilst not primarily concerned with environmental protection will give greater consideration to issues such as energy efficiency and the use of environmentally friendly building materials.
- Construction operations must be carried out in such a manner so as to cause no unavoidable pollution of the air, land or water.
- Waste materials must be disposed of in accordance with the new duty of care imposed by the EPA, and only by registered contractors.
- The government plan a new, comprehensive Environment Agency, for England and Wales, but this is unlikely to be in place until 1994.

11.10 Environmental assessment

- A structured approach is necessary to appraise successfully the environmental impact of any building.

- There are a variety of ways to assess environmental performance from the creation of an environmental policy based upon the information in this book to the use of a proprietary assessment method.
- Building Research Establishment environmental assessment method (BREEAM) version 1/90 assesses the performance of new office schemes.
- BREEAM 2/91 assesses the environmental impact of new supermarkets and superstores.
- BREEAM 3/91 advises on the performance of new homes.
- Watts & Partners' environmental survey gives practical advice tailored to the requirements of specific clients and individual buildings.
- Environmental impact assessments are sometimes necessary when making a planning application.
- The National Home Energy Rating Scheme and the Starpoint Home Energy Labels are two British methods for assessing energy efficiency of homes. The bodies responsible for these schemes are now implementing the government's standard assessment procedure.
- The European Commission has a scheme for environmental labelling of products, including some building materials. Products with an 'ecolabel' are expected to appear from 1993.

11.11 Overall conclusions

Producing a strategy to mitigate the environmental impact of a building or development scheme requires an understanding of individual environmental topics, knowledge of how these issues affect property and comprehension of the interrelationships between the various issues. The aim of this book has been to meet this need.

Once there is an understanding of specific environmental impacts and the way that these affect buildings, thought must be given to the type of environmental assessment which is appropriate in each situation. Chapter 10, on environmental assessment, introduces the different methods available. The off-the-peg methods, such as the BREEAM systems and energy labelling schemes, are undoubtedly useful in educating the market about environmental issues and allowing comparison of different buildings. Nevertheless, many will require a bespoke environmental assessment tailored to their specific requirements and those of their buildings. One possible way of approaching the development of a bespoke environmental strategy is given here.

As with communicating any other requirements, it is essential to set out the requirements clearly and concisely. In order to do this, a two-tier approach is suggested. First, the establishment of an environmental policy and, secondly, setting out environmental performance criteria.

The policy should be a simple statement which encapsulates the environmental objectives. As has been stressed earlier in this chapter, it is important to realise that there are no standard environmental solutions; therefore, any policy must take into account the unique features of the building, reflect the aims of those setting the strategy and attempt to anticipate the likely requirements of anyone who may acquire an interest in the building at some time in the future, such as a potential occupier. The need to predict future owner's requirements applies even where a building is being designed with a specific occupant in mind (rather than as a speculative development) in order to maximise the property's attractiveness should it ever become available on the open market. The policy could be as simple as 'the building will create a healthy environment for occupiers, meet current and anticipated environmental legislation and minimise pollution'.

Separate environmental performance criteria will be required for each topic in order to stipulate the action to be taken. These statements will need to be carefully considered so that they relate directly to the building in question and the aims of those establishing the policy. By taking this approach, one would avoid the risk of imposing potentially inappropriate standard solutions.

The number and type of environmental performance criteria will vary to suit individual buildings. However, a structured approach is necessary to minimise the chances of unintentionally omitting specific issues. A suggested approach is to think of environmental issues as falling into two groups: the internal and external environment. Topics within the internal environment are those that affect the quality of the environment within a building and tend to be health and safety issues. Examples include sick building syndrome and the environmental consequences of choosing particular building materials such as solvent-based paints. The second group of issues fall under the heading of the external environment. These are issues which arise from a building and affect the neighbourhood or global environment. Examples include the use of ozone-depleting chlorofluorocarbons and buildings with a short design life which implies poor use of finite building materials.

Establishing an environmental strategy is undoubtedly important, but it would be useless if it is not implemented. Therefore, a successful assessment requires monitoring, and review and revision of the policy and performance criteria from time to time. It is naïve to expect any policy or criteria to be implemented without monitoring.

Index

Abatement notices 154
Acid rain 115–16, 67
Acoustics 59–61
Actinomycetes 131–2
Advanced building management systems 113
Aims of the book 1–2
Air-borne allergies 136
Air diffusion performance index 111
Air pollution 153–5
Air pollution control 153
Algae 132
Allergic illness 136–7
Allergic rhinitis 137
Anobium punctatum 133
Aromatherapy 112
Asbestos 93–4
ASHRAE 111
Asthma 137
Atria 50

Bacteria 131, 136
Barrier, cut-off 28–30
Barrier, membrane 28–30
Bespoke environmental assessment 161, 181–2
Biodeterioration 122, 139
Biological balance 124
Biological decay 125–36
Biological health hazards 136–8
Biological agents 122, 139
Birds 134–5
BREEAM assessment systems 62, 161–5
Breathing zone filtration 114
British Standards Institution 22, 161
Bronchopulmonary aspergillosis 137–8
Building biology 122

Building environments 123–5
Building Research Establishment 37, 48, 77, 161
Building regulations 69–70, 150
Building-related illness 137
Building services engineering 53–6, 105

Cancer, lung 30, 34–5
Carbon dioxide 12, 28, 67, 90, 113
Carbon dioxide (CO_2) particles, body odours, and micro-organisms 113–14
CFC-blown insulants 92–3
Chlorofluorocarbons (CFCs) 9–15, 92–3, 115
CIBSE 112
Civil liability for pollution 155
Comfort conditions 110–11
Common furniture beetle 133
Computer-aided facilities diagnostics 108
Concrete 47
Consents for discharge of trade effluent 151–2
Construction Industry Research and Information Association (CIRIA) 26
Contaminated land 20–6, 148–9
Contaminative use, defined 149
Contributors to the book 5–7
Control of personal environments 109–10
Control of Substances Hazardous to Health (COSHH) Regulations 1988 21, 94, 96, 97
Cornwall 36

Damp houses 136
Deathwatch beetle 133–4

Demolition of buildings   157
Department of the Environment   22, 23, 146, 147, 153
Design life of buildings   74–5
Development plans   145–6
Direct Expansion [DX] Heat Pump System   78
Displacement ventilation   113
Dose, absorbed   32
Dose equivalent   33
Dry rot   125–7
Durability   74
Duty of care (waste)   152–3
Dynamic complex system   124

Ecological niches   122
Effective draught temperature   111
Energy labelling   167–9
Energy efficiency   67–8
Energy savings in building systems   75–6
Environment, legally defined   145
Environmental assessment   138–9, 146–8, 160–71
Environmental control   139–40
Environmental engineering   105
Environmental impact assessments   146–8, 167
Environmental moderating systems   77
Environmental performance   61–3, 106
Environmental policies   160–1, 181–2
Environmental Protection Act 1990   21, 144, 145, 148–9, 152, 153–4
Environmental protection agency   157
Environmental psychology   107
Environmental surveys   165–6
Epidemiology   38
Equipment gain   76, 78–9
European Community   157–8, 167, 169
Evaporative cooling   46
Exposure   34
External wall   56–8
Extremely low-frequency (ELF) fields   37

Fan coil unit (FCU) systems   78
Feral pigeons   135

Flexibility   74–5
Floor, suspended   36–37
Formaldehyde   98–9, 137
Formaldehyde in processed timber boards   99
Fresh air purging   113
Fruit body   126
Fungal spores   125

Gas works   22, 149
Glare   46
Global warming   12–15, 67, 90
Greenhouse gases   12–15
Groundwater   26

Halon   11–12
Hazard, environmental   20
Health and safety legislation   155–6
Heating/ventilating/air-conditioning (HVAC) systems   77–9, 114
Heat loads   79–81
HEPA filter   114
'Hidden' energy costs   74
Holistic approach   79–81
House longhorn beetle   134
Hydrochlorofluorocarbons (HCFCs)   11, 93
Hydrofluorocarbons (HFCs)   11
Hypersensitivity pneumonitis   137

Indoor pollution levels   113–14
Insects   132–4
Institution of Environmental Health Officers   22
Internal environment   17, 105–6
Isolating bearings   59

Landfill gas   26–30
Landscape   45–6
Leachate   28
Lead-based paints   96–7
Leaf cutter bees   134
Legionnaires' disease   17, 115, 136
Leptospirosis   138
Leukaemia   38
Lichens   132
Life cycle costing   62, 82–5
Lighting   53–6, 77
Local materials   73

Methane   12, 28
Micro-climate   46, 122

Microwaves 38
Migration, of gas 28
Minimum outside air ventilation
    rate 112
Mites 136
Monitoring, of gas 29
Montreal Protocol 11
Mosses 132
Moulds 128–9, 136
Murine typhus fever 138

National Home Energy Rating
    Scheme 168
National Rivers Authority 21, 147,
    151
Natural ventilation 111–12
Night-time purging 77, 119
Noise 59–61, 150–1

Office equipment 113
Office planning 53
Orientation 46–7
Out-of-town schemes 75
Ozone depletion 9–12, 92

Pesticides 97, 139
Peziza spp 130
Plague 138
Planning permission 148
Plaster fungi 130
Pollution, legally defined 145
Powder post beetles 134
Power lines, overhead 37–9
Problem buildings 107
Processed tropical hardwood
    boards 92
Product labelling 169
Ptilinus beetle 134

Radar 38
Radioactivity 31
Radon 30–7
Rat bite fever 138
Recycled materials 99–100
Registered carriers of waste 152–3
Registers s.143 EPA 21, 148–9
Remediation 26
Responsible buildings 114
Rhizomorphs 125, 127
Risk, environmental 20
Rodents 134–5

Salmonellosis 138
Sampling 22–4
Sea Ranch 46
Serpula lacrymans 125–7
Sewers, discharges into 151–2
Shading of glazed areas 58, 105
Sick building syndrome 107–8, 137
Site investigation 23–6
Site planning 45–6
Slime moulds 129
Soft rot 127–8
Soil 23
Soil gas 29
Solitary wasp 134
Solvent-based paints 94–6
Stain fungi 130–1
Starpoint Home Energy Labels
    168–9
Statutory nuisance 153–5
Structure of the book 2–4
Suicide 37
Sulphur dioxide 15–16, 67
Summer comfort conditions 111
Sump, radon 36
Sun screening 58, 105
Sustainable development 144
Sustainable sources of timber 90–2
Sycamore 135

Tenebrionid beetle 134
Termites 134
Thermal comfort criteria 110–11
Thermal envelope 105
Thermal insulation 69–73
Thermal moderating 77, 114–19
Thermal storage effects of building
    construction 47, 77, 119
This Common Inheritance, Govern-
    ment White Paper 68, 144–5
Timber treatments 97–8
Timber 90–2
Total value of the building 68
Town and Country Planning
    Acts 145–8, 156
Trees 46, 134–6
Trichinosis 138
Trigger concentration 24–6
Tropical hardwoods 90–2

U values 58, 62, 69–70
Unitary heat pump (UHP)
    system 78

Uranium   31
Urea formaldehyde foam cavity
   insulation   98–9
Using the book   4–5

Variable air volume (VAV)
   systems   77–8
Variable refrigerant volume (VRV)
   multi-system heat pump   79
Ventilation and indoor air
   quality   111–12
Venting, of gas   28–30
Virus   137–8
Volatile organic compounds   137

Wall:floor ratio   49, 52

Waste disposal authority   28
Waste on land   152–3
Water pollution   151–2
Water Resources Act 1991   21, 151
Water, surface   23
Water-based paints   95–6
Wet rot   127
Wharf borer beetle   134
Winter comfort conditions   111
Wood preservatives   97–8, 139
Wood-boring weevils   134
Wood-boring insects   133–4
Woodworm   133
Working level month (WLM)   34

Xestobium rofovillosum   133–4